MARGARITAS

FROZEN, SPICY, AND BUBBLY—
OVER 100 DRINKS FOR EVERYONE!

MARGARITAS

FROZEN, SPICY, AND BUBBLY—
OVER 100 DRINKS FOR EVERYONE!

MAMIE FENNIMORE

CIDER MILL
PRESS

BOOK
PUBLISHERS
KENNEBUNKPORT, MAINE

Contents

Introduction

Cocktails are booming in major cities across the globe thanks to a new focus on craft spirits and quality ingredients. Another aspect of this movement is an embrace of classic libations. Bartenders everywhere are digging out old-school recipes and reinventing. The gin martini is finally back. Manhattans are on fire again (literally). And, with the resurgence of Cognac, the Sidecar has latched itself onto seemingly every drink list out there.

One spirit that has been granted new life by this look back to the classics is tequila. Best known as the main ingredient in a margarita, tequila has recently zoomed to the top of the trendy list. Connoisseurs are seeking out premium tequilas and mezcals. And many of these premium bottles are so good that patrons are choosing to sip them neat, or on the rocks. Like so many other spirits, the tequila world is increasingly valuing quality over quantity.

Tequila, like champagne, is a designated Appellation of Origin (AO) and can only be produced in the designated region of Tequila, which includes the city of the same name, Jalisco, Guanajuato, Michoacan, Nayarit, and Tamaulipas.

This regional product is tended to by individuals known as *jimadors*, who have taken great pains to learn this centuries-old art, which is still largely done by hand. In order to get a product that is saleable, these jimadors have to plant the agave, carefully tend to it, and harvest them when they are perfectly ripe.

Rest assured: a huge amount of time, energy, and passion gets put into every bottle of pure blue agave tequila. That's even more the case when the tequila is aged to reposado, anejo, and extra anejo status.

Tequila and mezcal are finally rising up and claiming spots on bars in the home and in the cocktail world. And they seem to be there to stay. With that in mind, I present this collection of recipes, hoping that it will help these wonderful spirits gain respect while still maintaining their famously fun personas.

THE ORIGIN OF THE MARGARITA

The origin of the margarita is a bit murky, as there are a few different stories floating around the industry. Some are glamorous tales featuring beautiful women bearing the name, allegories of actors and models, and stories of simple bar experimentation.

And even though the word makes almost everyone think of Mexico, it was probably born far away from there. The traditional way to consume tequila in Mexico is neat, served in a tall shot glass alongside another tall shot glass full of sangrita, a mixture of citrus, fruit syrup, and sometimes hot chili. The idea is alternate sips of the two, with the sangrita both cutting the tequila's bite and enhancing its fruitiness.

So if this classic cocktail isn't Mexican, where did it come from? The most plausible story claims that the margarita is a variation of a drink called The Daisy, which features the citrus and syrup that the margarita is famous for, but includes brandy instead of tequila. And, strangely enough, *margarita* is the Spanish word for "daisy flower."

This bit of information seems to shed light on the genesis of this cocktail, but I'm sure there are wilder tales about its origin floating around. Wherever it got its start, it came to prominence in 1953, when *Esquire* featured it as the "Drink of the Month." Since then, it has climbed from its murky beginnings to a cocktail that inhabits the fantasies of millions.

TYPES OF TEQUILA

Plata: Also called blanco, silver, joven, or white tequila, this is the purest form of distilled blue agave. Once it has been distilled, it is immediately bottled and distributed. Plata should taste fresh and fruity, with a clean, herbaceous hint. The best way to imbibe plata is on the rocks with a squeeze of fresh lime. Be sure to seek out premium tequila if you plan to try this method.

Mezcal: All tequila is mezcal. But not all mezcal is tequila. There are about 30 different varietals of the agave plant (*tobala* and *espadin* are two of the main varietals besides blue agave) that can be harvested, cooked, and distilled to make mezcal. Only one type can be used for tequila: blue agave. Keep an eye out for mixtos, which are not 100 percent pure blue agave. Most people experience mixtos when they are introduced to tequila, since there are more mixto brands on the market than pure agave brands. Legally, these mixto tequilas must be made with at least 51% pure blue agave sugar. The other half of the sugars can be from non-agave sources like cane sugar, which will affect the taste and experience of the spirit in a negative fashion. So, in order to make sure you're getting the best experience, carefully read the label of any tequila bottle before you purchase, and remember to say no to mixtos.

Reposado: This "rested" tequila is plata that has been aged in wooden barrels for a minimum of two months, but less than one year. This brief rest allows the tequila to mellow out, and adds just a hint of flavor. While imbibing a reposado, one may pick up on light notes of wood, vanilla, baking spices, and fruit.

Anejo: This "aged" tequila sits for a minimum of one year in wooden barrels, and for no more than three years. Anejo tequila has more depth and complexity than both plata and reposado, featuring notes of wood, nuts, and chocolate. While each brand is unique in terms of wood used and resting time, all anejo is going to be soft, smooth, and distinct on the palate.

Extra Anejo: This style is exactly what it sounds like: extra aged. The minimum is three years in oak barrels. It's also a relative newcomer to the scene—extra anejo only became an official classification in March 2006.

Flavored tequila: There are all sorts of flavored and infused tequilas on the market. Just going off the top of my head, I've seen espresso, cucumber, pomegranate, cinnamon, strawberry, coconut, and habanero. If you can think of it, there's a good chance there's a tequila that's made with it. Some of these are good when making cocktails, but be cautious, and always make sure to taste the tequila on its own first. Not all of the flavored tequilas are great. If you have the time, making your own infused tequila is a cool experiment. Once you get it down, they make for great gifts and are also welcome at any party.

> TIP: GARNISHING A RIM WITH SALT IS UP TO YOU! IF SALTING THE RIM, RUB A LIME OR YOUR PREFERRED CITRUS AROUND THE RIM OF THE GLASS FIRST TO HELP THE SALT STICK.

GLASSWARE

Rocks glass: This short and stout vessel is traditionally used for brown spirits such as whiskey and bourbon. But their versatility allows them to convey anything neat or over ice. A must-have for any home bar.

Classic margarita coupe: The margarita glass is similar to a champagne coupe, featuring the same wide mouth and just a bit more depth. Usually these glasses are used to serve frozen margaritas, but if you have some on the smaller side and are in a more formal setting, you may want to use them to serve the margarita straight up.

Cocktail glass: This one is famous due to its association with the martini. But it is also great for any of the straight-up margaritas in this collection, and an easy way to turn your party into a more elegant affair. If you're going to use these, be sure to chill them before using.

Collins glass: Tall and thin, this glass is intended for cocktails that have been poured over ice. As the mouth of this glass is narrow, keep some straws on hand if you're using them.

Mason jar: These are great if you're gunning for a more rustic, casual feel. Traditionally used for canning, their hardiness and versatility have vaulted them to everyday glassware status. I use them for water, juice, beer, and cocktails.

Shot glass: This little glass is meant to measure different spirits and liqueurs for cocktails, but is more commonly used for a shot of said spirit. And tequila just might be the most popular spirit gulped out of this tiny vessel. If you want to enjoy tequila this way, try bookending the shot with salt and lime.

Red Solo Cup: Don't laugh. These are great to fill with frozen margaritas at an outdoor party!!

Snifter: Traditionally used for brandy and cognac, as its wide base and narrow mouth allows oxygen to open up the spirit and concentrate its aromas at the top. Anejo and extra anejo tequilas are perfect for a snifter, as you're looking to pick up on all the nuances provided by the aged agave and oak.

TOOLS

Cocktail shaker: The best shaker is the Boston Shaker. It is simple, affordable, and utilitarian. Shake any cocktail in it and you will meet with success. There are other cocktail shakers with just one metal or glass cup and lids with the strainer built in. While these look nice, they jam easily and don't allow as much space for the cocktail to be shaken.

Strainer: The only strainer you need for your home bar is the Hawthorne Strainer. It is versatile and effective, fitting a few different-sized glasses.

Blender: This is essential when making any frozen cocktail. Before purchasing one, make sure it can crush ice into pieces small enough to pass through a straw. This is crucial for frozen margaritas, which require a slushy consistency.

Citrus juicer: A fork can do the trick, but a wooden or metal citrus reamer works even better. And an automatic juicer trumps them all, cutting out a ton of the labor and time needed to put on a top-notch party. Whatever weapon you choose, keep in mind that freshly squeezed juices are an absolute must for quality margaritas.

Measuring cups/jigger: Mixing cocktails is a science, which is one reason why professionals refer to it as mixology. And, as with any science, exact measurements are important when quality and consistency are the goals. These tools will help you be as precise as you need to be.

Bar spoon: The bar spoon is longer than your average soup or yogurt spoon, making it ideal for stirred cocktails served in tall Collins glasses. The shaft of the spoon is thin and spiraled, allowing you to get around any ice cubes for a more even, consistent stir. Bar spoons may seem unnecessary in the grand scheme of things, but trust me— they are truly the right tool for the job!

Simple Syrup

A key ingredient in a majority of cocktails out there, simple syrup is certainly worth learning how to make at home. Don't worry—the beauty of nearly every simple syrup recipe is evident right there in the name: simplicity! At its core, simple syrup is a 1:1, sugar:water ratio. Heat this combo in a saucepan until all of the sugar has dissolved, and you are left with a supersaturated sugar solution—aka syrup. From there, any cocktail is possible, since simple syrup is incredibly easy to flavor. Add any herb, spice, flower, or fruit to the mixture while it is heating and all of the flavor will be infused into the syrup.

Combine sugar and water in a medium saucepan and cook over medium heat until sugar is completely dissolved. Remove from heat, let cool, and store in the refrigerator until ready to use.

Variations: Add herbs, fruits, and vegetables to experiment with flavored simple syrups. Some of my favorite infused syrups feature thyme, lavender, rosemary, lemon peel, cinnamon sticks, whole cloves, red chili flakes, jalapeños, tarragon, basil, cilantro, black pepper, pink peppercorns, blueberries, or strawberries.

INGREDIENTS

1 cup sugar

1 cup water

On the Rocks

"On the Rocks" is a classic phrase in the spirits world, especially when it comes to margaritas. Before making your way through these recipes, please keep in mind that the "rocks," or ice, can make or break your drink. If you don't use thick ice cubes directly from the freezer, your drink will become diluted too quickly. Once this happens, it doesn't matter how good your other ingredients are—all that quality will be washed away.

The Classic Margarita

If you are craving a margarita, make this one. This one also provides a good place to jump off from and start experimenting.

1 Fill a Boston Shaker about halfway with ice. Add tequila, lime juice, simple syrup, and orange liqueur and shake vigorously until well-combined.

2 Rub the lime wedge around the rim of a rocks glass and then dip the rim in sea salt. Fill the glass with ice and strain the margarita into the glass. Place the lime wedge on the rim and serve!

Variation: Try using a smoky mezcal to add a completely different complexity to the standard recipe.

INGREDIENTS

2 oz. tequila plata

1 oz. freshly squeezed lime juice

¾ oz. simple syrup

1 oz. orange liqueur (Triple Sec, Cointreau, or Grand Marnier)

Sea salt for the rim

1 wedge of lime for the rim

The Simple Margarita

YIELD: 1 DRINK

Being a purist, sometimes I like a margarita without the orange liqueur. If you're intrigued by this recipe, be sure to use a premium tequila, as there is not much to mask the strong bite of a mixto.

INGREDIENTS

2 oz. tequila plata

1 oz. freshly squeezed lime juice

1 oz. simple syrup

Sea salt for the rim

1 wedge of lime for the rim

1 Fill a Boston Shaker about halfway with ice. Add tequila, lime juice, and simple syrup, and shake vigorously until well-combined.

2 Rub the lime wedge around the rim of a rocks glass and then dip the rim in sea salt. Fill the glass to the top with ice and strain the margarita into the glass. Place the lime wedge on the rim and serve!

Lemon-Lime Margarita

The combination of lemon and lime is one of a kind, and I love paring these two together. Fresh lemon brightens up any drink, while fresh lime adds a pleasant, sour bite. Together, they make magic..

1 Fill a Boston Shaker about halfway with ice. Add tequila, lime juice, lemon juice, and simple syrup, and shake vigorously until well-combined.

2 Rub the lime or lemon wedge around the rim of a rocks glass and then dip the rim in sea salt. Fill the glass to the top with ice and strain the margarita into the glass. Place the wedge of citrus on the rim and serve!

INGREDIENTS

2 oz. tequila plata

½ oz. freshly squeezed lime juice

½ oz. freshly squeezed lemon juice

1 oz. simple syrup

Sea salt for the rim

1 wedge of lime or lemon for the rim

Lemon Margarita

YIELD: 1 DRINK

There is nothing quite like fresh lemonade to quench that summer thirst. Add tequila when 5 p.m. rolls around, and you've thrown together the easiest happy hour ever.

INGREDIENTS

2 oz. tequila plata

1 oz. freshly squeezed lemon juice

1 oz. orange liqueur (Triple Sec, Cointreau, or Grand Marnier)

1 oz. simple syrup

Sea salt for the rim

1 wedge of lemon for the rim

1 Fill a Boston Shaker about halfway with ice. Add tequila, lemon juice, orange liqueur, and simple syrup, and shake vigorously until well-combined.

2 Rub the lemon wedge around the rim of a rocks glass and then dip the rim in sea salt. Fill the glass to the top with ice and strain the margarita into the glass. Place the lemon wedge on the rim and serve!

Black Pepper Margarita

I am a huge fan of freshly ground black pepper. I think it makes or breaks a meal. My love for this everyday spice inspired this margarita, where the spice of the black pepper is a perfect complement to the herbaceous quality of the tequila.

1 To make the simple syrup: See simple syrup recipe on Page 15. When syrup is boiling, add one teaspoon of whole black peppercorns and let them boil in the syrup for one minute. Remove saucepan from heat and allow the peppercorns to cool in the syrup.

2 Fill a Boston Shaker about halfway with clean ice. Add tequila, lime juice, lemon juice, and black pepper-infused simple syrup, and shake vigorously until well-combined.

3 Rub the lime wedge around the rim of a rocks glass and then dip the rim of the glass in the sea salt and ground black pepper. Fill the glass with ice and strain the margarita into the glass. Place the lemon wedge on the rim and serve!

INGREDIENTS

2 oz. tequila plata

½ oz. freshly squeezed lime juice

½ oz. freshly squeezed lemon juice

1 oz. black pepper-infused simple syrup

Sea salt for the rim

Freshly ground black pepper for the rim

1 wedge of lemon for the rim

Pomegranate Margarita

Pomegranate is high in antioxidants and features a perfect tartness. If you're looking for a healthier margarita option, try this one out. Plus, it's pretty good looking in the glass.

INGREDIENTS

2 oz. tequila reposado or pomegranate tequila

1½ oz. pomegranate juice

1 oz. freshly squeezed lime juice

²/₃ oz. simple syrup or grenadine

Sea salt for the rim

1 wedge of lime for the rim

Pomegranate seeds for garnish

1 Fill a Boston Shaker about halfway with ice. Add the tequila, pomegranate juice, lime juice, and simple syrup/grenadine, and shake vigorously until well-combined.

2 Rub the lime wedge around the rim of a rocks glass and then dip the rim of the glass in sea salt. Fill the glass to the top with ice and strain the margarita into the glass. Place the lime wedge on the rim, sprinkle the pomegranate seeds on top, and serve!

Pear Cinnamon Margarita

YIELD: 1 DRINK

I love the combination of pear and cinnamon in the fall and winter. Muddling fresh ginger adds an additional layer of fresh, spicy flavor, making this one of my favorites!

1 Add the ginger and lemon juice to a Boston Shaker and muddle.

2 Add ice, tequila, pear puree, and ginger liqueur to the shaker, and shake vigorously until well-combined.

3 Wet the rim of a rocks glass and then dip the rim in the cinnamon. Fill the glass with ice, strain the margarita into the glass, top with the splash of seltzer, and serve.

INGREDIENTS

2 oz. tequila reposado

1½ oz. fresh pear puree

1 oz. freshly squeezed lemon juice

1 inch of fresh ginger root, peeled

1 oz. Domaine de Canton, or other ginger-flavored liqueur

Splash of seltzer water

Cinnamon for the rim

Key Lime Margarita

YIELD: 1 DRINK

Key limes are famously used in pies. But these little limes, which are higher in acid and have a much more potent aroma than conventional limes, are used in Mexico in all citrus-based cocktails. So if you are interested in experiencing the spirit of Mexico, it is best to use key lime juice!

INGREDIENTS

2 oz. tequila plata

1 oz. freshly squeezed key lime juice

1 oz. orange liqueur (Triple Sec, Cointreau, or Grand Marnier)

1 oz. simple syrup

Sea salt for the rim

1 wedge of key lime for the rim

1 Fill a Boston Shaker about halfway with ice. Add tequila, key lime juice, orange liqueur, and simple syrup, and shake vigorously until well-combined.

2 Rub the key lime wedge around the rim of a rocks glass and then dip the rim in sea salt. Fill the glass to the top with ice and strain the margarita into the glass. Place the key lime wedge on the rim and serve!

Tip: A key lime is ripe when it is almost completely yellow. You may find them green at the store, so make sure you let these little guys ripen before using them.

Blood Orange Margarita

When I'm after a dramatic-looking drink, I love using blood oranges. Their deep red color turns any cocktail into a stunner.

1 Fill a Boston Shaker about halfway with ice. Add tequila, blood orange juice, orange liqueur, and simple syrup, and shake vigorously until well-combined.

2 Rub the blood orange wedge around the rim of a cocktail or rocks glass and then dip the rim in sea salt. Fill the glass to the top with ice and strain the margarita into the glass. Place the blood orange wedge on the rim and serve!

INGREDIENTS

2 oz. tequila plata

2 oz. freshly squeezed blood orange juice

½ oz. orange liqueur (Triple Sec, Cointreau, or Grand Marnier)

1 oz. simple syrup

Sea salt for the rim

1 wedge of blood orange for the rim

TIP: Looking for the best way to juice strawberries? Toss them with just a sprinkle of sugar and the juice of half a lime, and then use a fork to crush the berries. Let this mixture stand for five minutes, then puree the mixture in a food processor or blender. Strain through a fine mesh sieve and you have fresh strawberry juice!

Strawberry Margarita

YIELD: 1 DRINK

The sweetness of strawberry is a lovely counter to tequila's famous bite. Try this one and see if you don't feel just a bit more light hearted.

INGREDIENTS

2 oz. tequila plata

1 oz. strawberry-infused tequila

2 oz. freshly squeezed strawberry juice

1 oz. freshly squeezed lime juice

1 oz. simple syrup

Sea salt for the rim

1 wedge of lime for the rim

Small strawberry for garnish

1 Fill a Boston Shaker about halfway with ice. Add the tequila, strawberry-infused tequila, strawberry juice, lime juice, and simple syrup, and shake vigorously until well-combined.

2 Rub the lime wedge around the rim of a rocks glass and then dip the rim in sea salt. Fill the glass with ice and strain the margarita into the glass. Place the lime wedge and strawberry on the rim and serve!

Variation: Add rhubarb to your strawberry margarita to bring the classic dessert to your glass. To do this, make a rhubarb simple syrup! Use the simple syrup recipe on Page 15. When the sugar has dissolved and the syrup is boiling, place three stalks of diced rhubarb in the saucepan. After 5–8 minutes, or when the rhubarb is tender, remove the saucepan from the heat and allow the rhubarb to cool with the syrup. When cool, remove the rhubarb and reheat the saucepan over medium heat. When the syrup is thick enough to coat the back of a spoon, remove from the heat.

Raspberry Margarita

Raspberries are my go-to fruit for the perfect flavor combination of tangy and sweet. Almost always perfectly ripe, raspberries offer the simple, bold flavor that guarantees a delicious margarita.

INGREDIENTS

2 oz. tequila plata

1 oz. Chambord, or other raspberry-flavored liqueur

1 oz. freshly squeezed lime juice

1 oz. simple syrup

6–8 fresh raspberries

Sea salt for the rim

1 wedge of lime for the rim

1 raspberry for garnish

Splash of seltzer, optional

1 Add the tequila and the raspberries to a Boston Shaker and muddle. Add ice, raspberry liqueur, lime juice, and simple syrup, and shake until well-combined.

2 Rub the rim of a rocks glass with the lime and then dip the rim in the salt. Fill glass with ice and strain margarita into glass. Top with a fizzy splash of seltzer if you like. Garnish with the lime wedge and the raspberry, and serve!

TIP: I know limes all seem the same in the store, but for margaritas—where freshly squeezed lime juice is essential to producing a quality cocktail—you want to make sure you are using RIPE limes. A ripe lime has a thin skin and seems heavier than it looks. Ripe limes feel like they have a lot of juice stored up inside, which they do. The juice of a mature lime is a bit sweeter and not as acidic. If you are making a few margaritas, try squeezing the lime juice out a few hours before mixing up the drinks. This allows for the lime juice to open up and mellow out. Try it out, and see if there is a difference!

Blackberry Margarita

I first fell in love with blackberries when I was a child picking them off the bush in my grandparents' back yard. Their perfect mix of sweet and tart made for a nice midday treat. At the end of the season we would make blackberry preserves. Recently, I thought of making cocktails with the fresh berries themselves (or the preserves), feeling that tequila and mezcal would complement the berries' flavor profile.

1 Add the tequila, mezcal, and blackberries to a Boston Shaker and muddle. Add ice, lime juice, and simple syrup, and shake until well-combined.

2 Rub the rim of a rocks glass with the lime and then dip the rim in sea salt. Fill glass with ice and strain the margarita into the glass. Top with a fizzy splash of seltzer if you like. Garnish with a lime wedge and a blackberry, and serve!

INGREDIENTS

2 oz. tequila plata

1 oz. mezcal

1 oz. freshly squeezed lime juice

1 oz. simple syrup

4–5 fresh blackberries

Sea salt for the rim

1 wedge of lime for the rim

1 blackberry for garnish

Splash of seltzer, optional

Cranberry Margarita

For those of you who do not harbor a sweet tooth, try a cranberry margarita. Cranberries' classic bitterness is perfect for a refreshing margarita, whether it's a hot summer evening or a festive holiday gathering.

INGREDIENTS

- 3 oz. tequila reposado
- 2 oz. cranberry juice (not cranberry cocktail)
- 1 oz. freshly squeezed lime juice
- 1 oz. simple syrup
- ½ oz. orange liqueur (Triple Sec, Cointreau, or Grand Marnier)
- Sea salt for the rim
- 1 wedge of lime for the rim
- Fresh cranberries for garnish

1 Fill a Boston Shaker about halfway with ice. Add tequila, cranberry juice, lime juice, simple syrup, and orange liqueur, and shake vigorously until well-combined.

2 Rub the lime wedge around the rim of a rocks glass and then dip the rim in sea salt. Fill the glass to the top with ice and strain the margarita into the glass. Place the lime wedge on the rim, garnish with cranberries, and serve!

TRIPLE SEC VS. COINTREAU VS. GRAND MARNIER

The main difference between these first two orange liqueurs is the ABV (alcohol by volume). The flavors are pretty similar, because Cointreau technically *is* Triple Sec. Triple Sec can range anywhere from 20–30% ABV, while Cointreau hikes it up to about 40%. Really, it is up to you which orange liqueur you want to use, but make sure you're always aware how much oomph your choice is going to provide. On a hot summer day it might be more economical to use an inexpensive Triple Sec, since people may be drinking faster. But when you're having an intimate cocktail party or just whipping one up for yourself, go for Cointreau. As for Grand Marnier, it is much more expensive than the other two because of its Cognac base. Grand Marnier has been aged, giving it notes of vanilla, candied orange peel, and toasted oak. There's no clear winner between the three. You just have to try them all and see which one fits your bill—who knows, it might be all three!

Basil Margarita

Whether it comes from the supermarket or comes fresh from your garden, basil is perhaps the most widely used household herb. Pair this common leafy herb with lime and tequila for an uncommonly refreshing margarita.

1 To make the simple syrup: See simple syrup recipe on Page 15. When syrup is boiling, add 5–7 basil leaves. After one minute, remove the saucepan from the heat and allow the basil leaves to cool with the syrup.

2 Fill a Boston Shaker about halfway with ice. Add tequila, lime juice, basil-infused simple syrup, and orange liqueur, and shake vigorously until well-combined.

3 Rub the lime wedge around the rim of a rocks glass and then dip the rim in sea salt. Fill the glass to the top with ice and strain the margarita into the glass. Place the lime wedge on the rim, garnish with a basil leaf, and serve!

INGREDIENTS

2 oz. tequila plata

1 oz. freshly squeezed lime juice

¾ oz. basil-infused simple syrup

1 oz. orange liqueur (Triple Sec, Cointreau, or Grand Marnier)

Sea salt for the rim

1 wedge of lime for the rim

Small basil leaves for garnish

Watermelon Margarita

Whatever form it appears in, watermelon is renowned for being the most thirst-quenching fruit. Remove the seeds and rind, puree the watermelon to your desired consistency, and this margarita will soon be your new favorite beverage!

INGREDIENTS

2 oz. tequila plata

1 oz. freshly squeezed lime juice

1½ oz. watermelon, cubed

½ oz. simple syrup

1 oz. orange liqueur (Triple Sec, Cointreau, or Grand Marnier)

Sea salt for the rim

1 wedge of lime for the rim

1 Place the watermelon in a blender or food processor and blend until smooth.

2 Fill a Boston Shaker about halfway with ice. Add tequila, lime juice, watermelon puree, simple syrup, and orange liqueur, and shake vigorously until well-combined.

3 Rub the lime wedge around the rim of a rocks glass and then dip the rim in sea salt. Fill the glass to the top with ice and strain the margarita into the glass. Place the lime wedge on the rim and serve!

Lavender Margarita

A classic flower of the south of France, lavender adds sweet and earthy notes to this margarita.

1 To make the simple syrup: See simple syrup recipe on Page 15. When syrup is boiling, add 5–7 sprigs of lavender. After one minute, remove the saucepan from the heat and allow the lavender to cool with the syrup.

2 Combine the tequila, orange liqueur, lavender-infused simple syrup, and lime juice in a Boston Shaker. Add ice and shake well.

3 Wet the rim of a rocks glass and then dip it in the sugar. Fill glass with ice and strain the margarita into the glass. Top with a fizzy splash of seltzer, if preferred. Garnish with a lime wedge or a sprig of fresh lavender, and serve!

INGREDIENTS

2 oz. tequila plata

½ oz. orange liqueur (Triple Sec, Cointreau, or Grand Marnier)

1 oz. lavender-infused simple syrup

1 oz. freshly squeezed lime juice

Sugar for the rim

Splash of seltzer, optional

1 sprig of lavender, optional

1 wedge of lime, optional

Thyme Margarita

YIELD: 1 DRINK

Thyme just might be my favorite herb to work with. Try this cocktail, and you'll see why.

INGREDIENTS

2 oz. tequila plata

½ oz. Yellow Chartreuse liqueur

1 oz. thyme-infused simple syrup

1 oz. freshly squeezed lime juice

Sea salt for the rim

1 teaspoon fresh thyme leaves, finely chopped

1 sprig of thyme, optional

1 wedge of lime, optional

1 To make the simple syrup: See simple syrup recipe on Page 15. When syrup is boiling, add 5–7 sprigs of thyme. After one minute, remove the saucepan from the heat and allow the thyme to cool with the syrup.

2 Combine the tequila, Yellow Chartreuse, thyme-infused simple syrup, and lime juice in a Boston Shaker. Add ice and shake well.

3 Combine the thyme leaves and sea salt in a small dish. Wet the rim of a rocks glass and then dip it into the salt-and-thyme mixture. Fill glass with ice and strain the margarita into the glass. Garnish with the lime wedge or the sprig of fresh thyme, and serve.

Rosemary Margarita

YIELD: 1 DRINK

Rosemary is a strong herb that reminds me of the holidays. Allow this hardy herb to star all year round!

1 To make the simple syrup: See simple syrup recipe on Page 15. When syrup is boiling, add 5–7 sprigs of rosemary. After one minute, remove the saucepan from the heat and allow the rosemary to cool with the syrup.

2 Combine the tequila, Yellow Chartreuse, rosemary-infused simple syrup, lime juice, and lemon juice in a Boston Shaker. Add ice and shake well.

3 Wet rim of rocks glass and dip it into the sugar. Fill glass with ice and strain the margarita into the glass. Garnish with the lime wedge or the sprig of rosemary, and serve.

INGREDIENTS

2 oz. tequila reposado

½ oz. Yellow Chartreuse liqueur

1 oz. rosemary-infused simple syrup

½ oz. freshly squeezed lime juice

½ oz. freshly squeezed lemon juice

Sugar for the rim

1 wedge of lime for garnish

1 sprig of rosemary for garnish

Mojito-rita

YIELD: 1 DRINK

Margarita or Mojito . . . mojito or margarita? Por que no los dos?! Life is better when you don't have to pick just one. By fusing the traditional Cuban rum cocktail—the Mojito—with the essentials of a margarita, you get the unbeatable Mojito-rita.

INGREDIENTS

4 oz. tequila reposado

2 oz. freshly squeezed lime juice

2 oz. mint-infused simple syrup or agave nectar

1 oz. orange liqueur (Triple Sec, Cointreau, or Grand Marnier)

12–15 mint leaves

Sea salt for the rim

1 wedge of lime for the rim

Splash of seltzer, optional

1 To make the simple syrup: See simple syrup recipe on Page 15. When syrup is boiling, add 5–7 mint leaves. After one minute, remove the saucepan from the heat and allow the mint to cool with the syrup.

2 Add the tequila and 6–7 mint leaves to a Boston Shaker and muddle. Add ice, lime juice, and mint-infused simple syrup, and shake until well-combined.

3 Wet the rim of a Collins glass or mason jar and then dip it into the salt. Fill the glass with ice, strain margarita into glass, and top with a fizzy splash of seltzer if you like. Garnish with a lime wedge or mint leaves, and serve!

The Maine Margarita

Freeze those blueberries you picked in the summertime and enjoy a fresh blueberry margarita all year. An added bonus of using frozen blueberries—they add another layer of chill without diluting your drink.

1 Add the lime juice and blueberries to a Boston Shaker and muddle. Add ice, tequila, agave nectar, and bitters, and shake until chilled and well-combined.

2 Wet the rim of a rocks glass and then dip it in the sea salt. Fill glass with ice, strain margarita into glass, and top with a fizzy splash of seltzer, if preferred. Garnish with mint and serve!

INGREDIENTS

2 oz. anejo tequila

1½ oz. freshly squeezed lime juice

2 tablespoons fresh blueberries

1 oz. agave nectar

2–3 dashes of orange bitters

Sea salt for the rim

Mint for garnish

Cucumber Mint Margarita

YIELD: 1 DRINK

Fresh and fresher. It does not get anymore refreshing than the mint-cucumber combo. A splash of seltzer water would be the cherry on top for this refreshing summer favorite.

INGREDIENTS

4 oz. tequila reposado

2 oz. freshly squeezed lime juice

2 oz. mint-infused simple syrup or agave nectar

12–15 mint leaves

1 tablespoon of cucumber, diced

Sea salt for the rim

1 wedge of lime

1 To make the simple syrup: See simple syrup recipe on Page 15. When syrup is boiling, add 5–7 mint leaves. After one minute, remove the saucepan from the heat and allow the mint to cool with the syrup.

2 Add the tequila, 1 heaping tablespoon of cucumber, and 2–3 mint leaves to a Boston Shaker and muddle. Add ice, lime juice, and mint-infused simple syrup, and shake until well-combined.

3 Wet the rim of your favorite cocktail glass and then dip it into the sea salt. Fill glass with ice and strain the margarita into the glass. Garnish with a lime wedge and mint leaves, and serve!

Rosemary-Ginger Margarita

Fresh ginger is so zingy, sometimes it needs another strong companion to round out its spiciness. Rosemary does the trick! The rosemary has enough presence to bring out all of the positive elements of the ginger (sweetness and warmth) while still retaining its classic piney flavor.

1 To make the simple syrup: See simple syrup recipe on Page 15. When syrup is boiling, add 5–7 sprigs of rosemary. After one minute, remove the saucepan from the heat and allow the rosemary to cool with the syrup.

2 Add the tequila, ginger liqueur, pieces of fresh ginger, lime juice, and lemon juice to a Boston Shaker and muddle.

3 Add rosemary-infused simple syrup and ice, and shake well.

4 Wet the rim of a rocks glass and then dip the rim in the salt. Fill the glass with ice, strain the margarita into the glass, garnish with the rosemary sprig and candied ginger, and serve.

INGREDIENTS

2 oz. tequila reposado

1 oz. Domaine de Canton, or other ginger-flavored liqueur

½ oz. rosemary-infused simple syrup

1–2 small pieces of fresh ginger root, peeled

½ oz. freshly squeezed lime juice

½ oz. freshly squeezed lemon juice

Sea salt for the rim

Candied ginger for garnish

1 sprig of rosemary for garnish

CANDIED GARNISHES

Candied garnishes are as impressive looking as they are toothsome. And candied citrus peels, herb leaves, and fruit slices are easier to make than it may seem. Some of my favorites are orange peels, sage leaves, and fresh ginger slices.

CANDIED GINGER: Peel a piece of fresh ginger root and slice into thin rounds (approximately one-eighth of an inch thick). Place the rounds in a medium saucepan, cover with water, and cook over medium heat until the ginger is tender, approximately 45 minutes to one hour. Make sure to add water and keep the ginger covered as it cooks. Drain, return the ginger to the saucepan with an equal amount of sugar and water, and cook over medium heat until it comes to a boil. After 10–15 minutes, remove saucepan from heat and allow the ginger to cool in the syrup for at least an hour, or overnight. Drain the ginger (if the syrup has hardened overnight, warm it over low heat until it is liquid again), toss pieces in granulated sugar, and place onto a greased cooling rack until dry.

CANDIED ORANGE PEEL: Remove the peel of an orange, taking care not to take too much of the white pith, as it tends to be bitter. Slice the peel into one-quarter inch slices, place into a saucepan, and cover with water. Bring to a boil, adding water to keep the pieces of peel covered. After 15–20 minutes, drain the strips of peel and rinse them. Combine two cups of sugar and two cups of water in another saucepan and boil until the sugar is completely dissolved. Add the orange peels to the syrup and cook over low heat for 40–45 minutes. Drain the peels, toss them in granulated sugar, and place them onto a greased cooling rack until dry. This method will work for the peel of any citrus fruit.

CANDIED SAGE LEAVES (OR MINT, BASIL, ETC.): Combine two cups of sugar and two cups of water in a medium saucepan and bring to a boil. Cook until all of the sugar is completely dissolved, remove from heat, and let cool. Wash and thoroughly dry whole, fresh sage leaves. Using a pastry brush, brush the cooled syrup on both sides of the sage leaves and then dip the leaves in granulated sugar. Place on a greased cooling rack and let cool for a few hours, or overnight. This method will also work for herbs such as mint or basil, so don't be afraid to experiment.

Aloe Vera Margarita

You may recognize aloe vera as something you apply in order to soothe a sunburn. Well, it not only refreshes your skin—it is also a refreshing, hydrating beverage. Make this margarita a summertime staple.

1 Fill a Boston Shaker about halfway with ice. Add tequila, aloe vera juice, lime juice, and agave nectar, and shake vigorously until chilled and well-combined.

2 Rub the lime wedge around the rim of a rocks glass and then dip the rim in sea salt. Fill the glass to the top with ice and strain the margarita into the glass. Place the lime wedge on the rim and serve!

INGREDIENTS

2 oz. tequila plata

2½ oz. aloe vera juice

1½ oz. freshly squeezed lime juice

¾ oz. agave nectar

Sea salt for the rim

1 wedge of lime for the rim

Elderflower Margarita

While you may not know what elderflower is, you have undoubtedly come across it on a cocktail menu. Elderflower liqueur comes from the elderberry and adds bright, beautiful flavor to any drink. This margarita is truly one of a kind!

INGREDIENTS

2 oz. tequila plata

2 oz. St-Germain or elderflower liqueur

1 ⅓ oz. freshly squeezed lime juice

Sea salt for the rim

1 wedge of lime for the rim

Splash of seltzer, optional

1 small, white flower, optional

1 Combine the tequila, St-Germain, and lime juice in a Boston Shaker. Add ice and shake until well-combined.

2 Rub the lime wedge around the rim of a cocktail glass and then dip the rim in sea salt. Fill the glass to the top with ice and strain the margarita into the glass. Top with a splash of seltzer, if preferred. Garnish with the lime wedge or flower, and serve!

Old Fashioned

This cocktail is one of the oldest drinks out there. Reinventing it with tequila and lime allows you to shake things up. But be sure not to shake this one! The Old Fashioned is stirred, always.

1 Combine the bitters and syrup in the bottom of a chilled rocks glass. Add the tequila and stir.

2 Add 1–2 medium ice cubes to the glass and stir for about 30–45 seconds. Garnish with the twist of lime and serve.

INGREDIENTS

2 oz. anejo tequila

½ oz. simple syrup

2–3 dashes orange bitters

1 twist of lime

Sherry Margarita

Be sure to use a good fino sherry in this recipe. It should be both complex and sweet, balancing out the tequila's bite and adding multiple layers to the margarita.

INGREDIENTS

1 oz. tequila plata

1 oz. Fino sherry

¾ oz. freshly squeezed grapefruit juice

½ oz. freshly squeezed lime juice

¼ oz. agave nectar

1–2 dashes of orange bitters

1 twist of lime for garnish

1 Fill a Boston Shaker about halfway with ice. Add all ingredients save the twist of lime, and shake until combined and very well-chilled.

2 Wet the rim of a rocks glass and dip the rim in sea salt. Fill the glass with ice and strain the margarita into the glass. Garnish with the twist of lime and serve.

TIP: Sherry tends to be an overwhelming purchase for most consumers, since it is not the most popular item on the scene at the moment. Sherry is mysterious enough to evade even the attention of a savvy winedrinker. But, like port, sherry is making a comeback! The main kinds of sherry are: Manzanilla, Fino, Amontillado, Pedro Ximenez, and cream. They are not the only varieties, but they are the ones you are most likely to come across. The exciting thing about sherry is the versatility offered by the different types: Fino and Manzanilla are dry and perfect for those margaritas that are citrusy; sweeter sherries, like Pedro Ximenez, are perfect for the margaritas that use anejo and extra anejo tequilas.

Morning Margarita

YIELD: 1 DRINK

Yes, a margarita in the morning! Serve this at your next brunch, it's a guaranteed eye-opener.

INGREDIENTS

2 oz. tequila reposado

2 teaspoons orange marmalade

1 oz. freshly squeezed lime juice

½ oz. simple syrup

½ oz. orange liqueur (Triple Sec, Cointreau, or Grand Marnier)

Sea salt for the rim

1 wedge of lime for the rim

Splash of seltzer, optional

1 twist of orange, optional

1 Combine the tequila, marmalade, lime juice, simple syrup, and orange liqueur in a Boston Shaker. Add ice and shake until well-combined.

2 Rub the lime wedge around the rim of a rocks glass and dip the rim in sea salt. Fill the rocks glass with ice and strain the margarita into the glass. Top with the splash of seltzer, if preferred. Garnish with the lime wedge or the twist of orange, and serve.

Margarita

Using mezcal will give the drink a deeper, more complex layer of smokiness. Try it both ways and see which one you prefer!

1 Combine 1 tablespoon sea salt with 1 teaspoon smoked paprika in a small bowl.

2 To make the simple syrup: See simple syrup recipe on Page 15. When syrup is boiling, add two ancho chilies. After one minute, remove the saucepan from the heat and allow the chilies to cool with the syrup.

3 Fill a Boston Shaker about halfway with ice. Add tequila, ancho chili-infused simple syrup, lime juice, and orange liqueur, and shake vigorously until well-combined.

4 Rub the lime wedge around the rim of a rocks glass and then dip the rim in the blend of salt and paprika. Fill the glass with ice and strain the margarita into the glass. Place the lemon wedge on the rim, and serve!

Variation: Use mezcal in place of tequila for an even smokier iteration.

INGREDIENTS

2 oz. tequila reposado

1 oz. ancho chili-infused simple syrup

1 oz. freshly squeezed lime juice

½ oz. orange liqueur (Triple Sec, Cointreau, or Grand Marnier)

1 tablespoon smoked sea salt

1 teaspoon smoked paprika

1 wedge of lime

Straight Up

Asking a bartender to serve you a cocktail "straight up" is simply requesting that they serve it in the proper glass, with no ice. As these cocktails focus more on the simple flavors of the actual booze, it is essential that the materials used are of the highest quality, since there is no melted ice to dilute the flavors. And sure, there is no "second drink" once the ice melts. But trust me—the first one will do the trick!

For the margaritas in this section, and most of the margaritas in this book, it is essential that you use a chilled glass. So make sure you place your glassware in the freezer a half-hour before you're going to use them.

HOMEMADE MARASCHINO CHERRIES

Trust me, these are much better than the standard brands you can buy in a store. If you don't feel like making them, try seeking out specialty stores for a more-artisanal brand. You'll taste the difference!

INGREDIENTS

1 lb. sweet, ripe cherries, stemmed and pitted

¾ cup sugar

2 tablespoons freshly squeezed lemon juice

¼ cup water

½ vanilla bean

1 cup Luxardo

1. Combine the water, sugar, and seeds of the vanilla bean in a medium saucepan and bring to a boil. Once the sugar has dissolved, simmer for 20 minutes. Add the lemon juice and simmer for 2–3 more minutes. Remove from heat and add the Luxardo.

2. After the syrup has cooled slightly, place the cherries and the vanilla bean in an insulated, air-tight container. Pour the warm syrup over the cherries and seal the container. Let sit in the refrigerator for at least 5–6 days before serving. Use the cherries and the juice for cocktails, desserts, or snacking.

Maraschino Cherry Margarita

If you're like me, you have a jar of maraschino cherries in your fridge, and no idea what to do with the juice. Obviously, you can always make a Shirley Temple or two. But I've discovered that the maraschino margarita is a gorgeous cocktail—both in look and taste.

1 To make the simple syrup: See simple syrup recipe on Page 15. When syrup is boiling, add 5–7 pieces of ginger. After one minute, remove the saucepan from the heat and allow the ginger to cool with the syrup.

2 Add the tequila, maraschino juice, Luxardo, ginger-infused simple syrup, lime juice, and ice to a Boston Shaker, and shake until combined and well-chilled.

3 Wet the rim of a martini glass or small margarita coupe and then dip the rim into the sea salt. Strain the cocktail into the glass, garnish with the maraschino cherries, and serve.

INGREDIENTS

2 oz. tequila plata

1½ oz. maraschino cherry juice

½ oz. Luxardo liqueur

½ oz. ginger-infused simple syrup

1 oz. freshly squeezed lime juice

Sea salt for the rim

1–2 maraschino cherries for garnish

Cuties Margarita

What to do with that box of clementines in the winter? Make a margarita, of course! The juice is light and sweet, and makes for a perfect wintertime treat.

INGREDIENTS

2 oz. tequila plata

2 oz. freshly squeezed clementine juice

½ oz. orange liqueur (Triple Sec, Cointreau, or Grand Marnier)

½ oz. simple syrup, optional (depending on sweetness of clementine juice)

Sea salt for the rim

1 wedge of clementine for the rim

1 Add the tequila, clementine juice, orange liqueur, simple syrup, and ice to a Boston Shaker, and shake until combined and well-chilled.

2 Wet the rim of a margarita coupe and then dip the rim into the sea salt. Strain the cocktail into the glass, garnish with the wedge of clementine, and serve.

The Tequila Daisy

Although there is a classic margarita recipe at the beginning of the book, this is the original. Keep this one as simple as you can, with no garnish.

1 Fill a Boston Shaker halfway with ice, add all the ingredients save the seltzer, and shake until well-chilled.

2 Strain into a small margarita coupe or martini glass. Top with the splash of seltzer water, and serve.

INGREDIENTS

2 oz. tequila plata or reposado

1 oz. freshly squeezed lemon juice

½ oz. grenadine

½ oz. simple syrup

Splash of seltzer

Sidecar

A classic cocktail that focuses entirely on the booze. Because of that, make sure you use a good anejo tequila.

INGREDIENTS

1½ oz. anejo tequila (if you can find one aged in old cognac barrels, even better)

1 oz. simple syrup

1 oz. orange liqueur (Triple Sec, Cointreau, or Grand Marnier)

½ oz. freshly squeezed lime juice

1 twist of lime for garnish

1 Fill a Boston Shaker halfway with ice, add all the ingredients, and shake until well-chilled.

2 Strain into a margarita coupe or martini glass. Garnish with the twist of lime, and serve.

Hibiscus Margarita

Hibiscus plants have been used to treat a wealth of maladies since Ancient Egypt. My favorite use for this tropical flower? Margaritas, of course! Steeping hibiscus tea helps me create my favorite floral treat.

1 Fill a Boston Shaker halfway with ice, add the tequila, tea, lime juice, orange liqueur, and agave nectar, and shake until chilled and well-combined.

2 Rub lime wedge around the rim of a martini glass or small margarita coupe and then dip the rim into the sea salt. Strain the cocktail into the glass, top with the splash of seltzer water, garnish with the lime wedge or a twist of lime peel, and serve.

INGREDIENTS

2 oz. tequila plata

1½ oz. hibiscus tea

1 oz. freshly squeezed lime juice

1 oz. orange liqueur (Triple Sec, Cointreau, or Grand Marnier)

½ oz. agave nectar

Sea salt for the rim

1 wedge of lime for the rim

1 twist of lime for garnish, optional

Splash of seltzer

Lychee Margarita

Serving the lychee margarita in a martini glass makes it extra special! Trust me, you and your friends will love trying this pink drink.

INGREDIENTS

8 oz. can of lychee

2 oz. tequila plata

1 oz. of lychee puree

1 oz. freshly squeezed lime juice

1 lychee

1 wedge of lime for the rim

Sugar or salt for the rim

Splash of seltzer water, optional

1 Make the lychee puree: Pour an eight ounce can of lychee and one-third of the syrup into a blender and blend until it is pureed.

2 Fill a Boston Shaker halfway with ice, add the tequila, lychee puree, and lime juice, and shake until well-chilled.

3 Rub the lime wedge around the rim of a small margarita coupe or martini glass and dip the glass in the sugar or salt. Strain the cocktail into the glass and top with the splash of seltzer, if preferred. Garnish with the lime wedge and the lychee, and serve.

Jalisco Sour

If you've ever heard of the Pisco Sour then you'll have a general idea where I'm headed. Pisco is a type of brandy made in Chile and Peru. It's typically used in a cocktail featuring a signature egg white foam, but I've adapted the recipe into a margarita. Its name comes from one of tequila's homes—Jalisco, Mexico.

1 Fill a Boston Shaker halfway with crushed ice, add all the ingredients save the nutmeg and Angostura bitters, and shake until well-chilled.

2 Strain into a small margarita coupe or martini glass and garnish with a lime wedge or twist of lime. Lightly grate nutmeg over the top, add the bitters, and serve.

INGREDIENTS

1 oz. tequila plata

1 oz. pisco

¾ oz. freshly squeezed lime juice

¾ oz. simple syrup

1 fresh egg white

Crushed ice

Grated nutmeg

3–4 dashes of Angostura bitters

1 wedge of lime, optional

1 twist of lime, optional

Honey Margarita

There are so many different types of honey available, so make sure you try out different kinds—like clover, orange blossom, eucalyptus, and sage—to see how each one changes the margarita's flavor.

INGREDIENTS

3 oz. anejo tequila (if you can find one aged in old cognac barrels, even better)

½ oz. simple syrup

½ oz. orange liqueur (Triple Sec, Cointreau, or Grand Marnier)

2 oz. honey

1 oz. freshly squeezed lime juice

Bee pollen for the rim

Sea salt for the rim

1 sprig of mint for garnish

1 Heat the simple syrup in a small saucepan, add the honey, and stir to combine. When both are heated, remove the saucepan from the heat and allow to cool.

2 Fill a Boston Shaker halfway with ice, add the tequila, honey/simple syrup mixture, orange liqueur, and lime juice, and shake until well-chilled.

3 Wet the rim of a martini glass and then dip it into the salt and bee pollen. Strain the cocktail into the glass, garnish with the mint, and serve.

Pink Peppercorn Grapefruit Margarita

YIELD: 1 DRINK

The hint of spice provided by the pink peppercorns is just enough to balance out the grapefruit's bitterness.

1 To make the simple syrup: See simple syrup recipe on Page 15. When syrup is boiling, add three tablespoons of pink peppercorns. After one minute, remove the saucepan from the heat and allow the peppercorns to cool with the syrup.

2 Combine the sea salt and ground pink peppercorns in a small bowl and set aside.

3 Fill a Boston Shaker halfway with ice, add the tequila, grapefruit juice, and pink peppercorn-infused syrup, and shake until well-combined.

4 Rub the wedge of grapefruit around the rim of a martini glass or margarita coupe and dip the rim into the pink peppercorn-salt mixture. Strain cocktail into the glass and top with a splash of seltzer, if preferred. Garnish with the wedge of grapefruit and serve.

INGREDIENTS

2 oz. tequila plata

3 oz. freshly squeezed grapefruit juice

1 oz. pink peppercorn-infused simple syrup (cook 3 tablespoons pink peppercorns in the simple syrup recipe)

Ground pink peppercorns for the rim

Sea salt for the rim

1 wedge of grapefruit for the rim

Splash of seltzer, optional

Gimlet

YIELD: 1 DRINK

The richness of the lime juice in this cocktail highlights the more subtle flavors of the tequila—just as it does in the classic gin version. It can be challenging to bring out the pure agave flavors in tequila, but this drink makes it easy.

INGREDIENTS

3 oz. tequila plata

1½ oz. freshly squeezed lime juice

1 wedge of lime for garnish

Splash of seltzer, optional

1 Fill a Boston Shaker halfway with ice. Add tequila and lime juice and shake until well-combined.

2 Strain margarita into a martini glass or a margarita coupe and top with a splash of seltzer, if preferred. Garnish with the lime wedge and serve.

Pear Cilantro Margarita

YIELD: 1 DRINK

Make your margarita stand out with the subtle infusion of fresh garden herbs. One of my favorite herby/fruity combinations is pear and cilantro. The pleasant, citrusy flavor of cilantro pairs well with sweet, ripe pears.

INGREDIENTS

1½ oz. tequila reposado

1½ oz. pear nectar

½ oz. agave nectar

1 oz. freshly squeezed lime juice

6–8 fresh cilantro leaves, minced

1 sprig of cilantro for garnish

Sea salt for the rim

1 wedge of lime for the rim

1 Add ice, tequila, pear nectar, agave nectar, lime juice, and cilantro to a Boston Shaker, and shake until combined and well-chilled.

2 Rub the rim of a margarita coupe with the lime and then dip the rim into the sea salt. Strain the margarita into the glass (it is okay if a few pieces of minced cilantro slip through), garnish with the sprig of cilantro, and serve.

Beet Margarita

I did not appreciate beets for the longest time. I thought they tasted like dirt, which they kind of do, and did not understand how anyone liked them. The first beet I truly enjoyed was pickled. The earthiness remained, but it was transformed by the salty, vinegar-y bite provided by the pickling. From that moment I loved beets raw, cooked, roasted, canned, you name it. This 180° spin of my palate inspired me to test out a beet margarita. Since beets provide wonderful color, I at least knew it would be a beautiful drink. To my surprise, they produced a genius margarita. The pickled beet margarita is on my top-three list from this entire collection. Try it and see!

1 Fill a Boston Shaker halfway with ice. Add the tequila, pickled beet juice, lime juice, and simple syrup, and shake until well-combined.

2 Wet the rim of a martini glass and dip it into salt. Strain margarita into the glass, and garnish with lime wedge and a skewer of pickled beets.

Variation: If you're looking for a more casual cocktail, this one is also great served over ice in a rocks glass.

INGREDIENTS

3 oz. tequila reposado

2 oz. pickled beet juice

2 oz. freshly squeezed lime juice

²/₃ oz. simple syrup

Sea salt for the rim

1 wedge of lime for the rim

Pickled beets for garnish

MEZCAL

There are all sorts of mezcal coming onto the market these days. In comparison to tequila, mezcal is much more rustic, both in cooking technique and flavor. The classic mezcal is incredibly smoky because the agave is slow-roasted over hot rocks in earthen ovens.

While there are many different varietals of agave used to produce mezcal, the most popular at the moment are: Espadin, Tobala, Tobaziche, Tepeztate, and Arroqueno. The first, Espadin, is the most common agave and the closest relative of blue agave, which is used exclusively in the production of tequila. Tobala is definitely the rarest of the agave varieties, and the most prestigious. Not many mezcal producers farm it, since it requires a certain altitude and soil to successfully grow, and it is harvested mostly from the wild. The last three varietals mentioned are also harvested in the wild.

As with wine, each type of agave has a terroir that can create starkly different mezcals. The soil, the climate, and environmental factors all contribute to the taste of the final product.

Maple Margarita

Be sure to use pure maple syrup in this recipe, since it's the star of the show. This one is perfect for a crisp autumn day.

1 Fill a Boston Shaker halfway with ice. Add all ingredients save the sea salt and citrus twist, and shake until chilled and well-combined.

2 Wet the rim of a martini glass or margarita coupe and dip it into the salt. Strain the margarita into the glass, garnish with the twist of lime or orange, and serve!

INGREDIENTS

1½ oz. tequila blanco

½ oz. orange liqueur

¼ oz. mezcal

1¼ oz. pure maple syrup

1 oz. freshly squeezed lime juice

Sea salt for the rim

1 twist of lime or orange for garnish

Guava Margarita

This delightful cocktail will have you going back for seconds. Guava has a tropical sweetness that you really cannot replicate. Despite this exoticness, it's not too tough to find—guava juices and nectars are now widely available in supermarkets.

INGREDIENTS

2 oz. tequila plata

2 oz. guava juice or nectar

1 oz. freshly squeezed lime juice

1 oz. orange liqueur (Triple Sec, Cointreau, or Grand Marnier)

½ oz. agave nectar

Sea salt for the rim

1 twist of lime for garnish, optional

1 ring of lime for garnish, optional

1 Fill a Boston Shaker halfway with ice. Add the tequila, guava juice, lime juice, orange liqueur, and agave nectar, and shake vigorously until combined and well-chilled.

2 Wet the rim of a martini glass or a small margarita coupe and dip it in the salt. Strain the margarita into the glass, garnish with a twist of lime or the ring of lime, and serve!

French Margarita

This one is perfect for those who are looking for something a little sweeter. That doesn't mean it's not complex though—it's more than tasty enough to tempt any martini lover!

1 Fill a Boston Shaker with ice. Add all ingredients, save the twist of lime, and shake until very well-chilled.

2 Strain the cocktail into a chilled martini glass, garnish with the lime twist, and serve.

INGREDIENTS

2 oz. tequila blanco

½ oz. pineapple juice

½ oz. freshly squeezed lime juice

¼ oz. Chambord or other raspberry-flavored liqueur

¼ oz. dry vermouth

1 twist of lime for garnish

Anticuado

When I first tasted this drink, I remember thinking that its balance of reposado and bitters provided the perfect update of the margarita. This one was inspired by mixologist Daniel Pidgeon at Pearl Restaurant in Kennebunk, Maine.

INGREDIENTS

1½ oz. tequila reposado

½ of a lime, cut into thirds

4½ dashes aromatic bitters

1 oz. freshly squeezed orange juice

½ oz. agave nectar

1 twist of lime for garnish

1 Add the tequila, lime, and bitters to a Boston Shaker and muddle. Add the orange juice, agave nectar, and ice, and shake vigorously until well-combined.

2 Double-strain the cocktail into a margarita coupe. Flame the lime peel, twist it, and use it as a garnish. Sit back and enjoy!

Flaming a lime peel:

When it comes to garnishes for margaritas, you can always add a wedge of fresh lime and be done with it. If you are feeling a little more adventurous, or you just want to have a fun party trick up your sleeve, try adding some fire to your garnish. Heating the lime, or even singeing it slightly with a flame, adds more flavor. Intrigued? Here's how: Peel a twist from a citrus peel, light a match, and hold the match under it until it is lightly brown and fragrant! You can use this technique for some herbs as well. Lightly burning herbs like rosemary or thyme adds a significant amount of flavor.

Up Against the Wall (Smoke on the Beach)

Sometimes mezcal provides a little too much smoke for my personal taste, but this cocktail uses pineapple to eliminate this issue. I cannot imagine a world without this combination! This one is also inspired by mixologist Daniel Pidgeon at Pearl Restaurant in Kennebunk, Maine.

1 Fill a Boston Shaker halfway with ice. Add all ingredients, save the orange peel, and shake until chilled and well-combined.

2 Double-strain the cocktail into a margarita coupe. Bend the orange peel over the glass to release the essential oils and aromas. Garnish cocktail with orange peel and serve.

INGREDIENTS

1 oz. mezcal

1 oz. tequila plata

1 oz. freshly squeezed lime juice

1 oz. pineapple juice, fresh or canned

½ oz. agave nectar

1 strip of orange peel for garnish

Amaro Margarita

Amaro is an herbal digestif traditionally consumed after dinner in Italy. It is syrupy, sweet, and has a complexity that keeps you thinking long after you've finished the glass. As I have fallen in love with amaro, I created this margarita. And to my surprise, it adds an element that I cannot create with any other ingredient.

INGREDIENTS

1½ oz. tequila reposado

½ oz. mescal

¾ oz. amaro

¾ oz. freshly squeezed lime juice

½ oz. agave nectar

1 slice of lime for garnish

1 Fill a Boston Shaker halfway with ice. Add all the ingredients save the slice of lime and shake until well-combined.

2 Double-strain the cocktail into a small margarita coupe or small martini glass. Garnish with the slice of lime and serve!

Tip: Be sure to use good amaro in this one. Nonino Quintessentia Amaro is my go-to.

Hot Toddy Margarita

Save this one for the coldest day of the year!! I guarantee you'll warm right up.

1 Combine the tequila, orange liqueur, agave nectar, lime juice, and orange juice in an insulated glass.

2 Top with the hot water, garnish with the cinnamon stick and cloves, and serve.

INGREDIENTS

2 oz. anejo tequila

¾ oz. orange liqueur (Triple Sec, Cointreau, or Grand Marnier)

½ oz. agave nectar

¼ oz. freshly squeezed lime juice

¼ oz. freshly squeezed orange juice

1 oz. hot water

1 cinnamon stick for garnish

1–2 whole cloves for garnish

Port Wine Margarita

Port has made quite a comeback thanks to the cocktail scene. And thank goodness, because ruby port adds great sweetness and color to any drink.

INGREDIENTS

1 oz. ruby port

2 oz. tequila plata

½ oz. fresh lime juice

1 oz. orange liqueur

½ oz. agave nectar

½ oz. fresh orange juice

Sea salt for the rim

1 twist of lime for garnish, optional

1 wedge of lime for garnish, optional

1 Fill a Boston Shaker about halfway with ice. Add the ruby port, tequila, lime juice, orange liqueur, agave nectar, and orange juice, and shake vigorously until well-combined.
2 Wet the rim of a small martini glass or margarita coupe and then dip the rim in sea salt. Strain cocktail into the glass, garnish with the twist of lime or the lime wedge, and serve.

Variation: Ruby vs. Tawny Port

Ruby ports are lively and fresh, and named for their beautiful color. These ports are great to use in cocktails that need more fruit or brightness. Ruby ports are generally affordable, making them great for beginners in the fortified wine scene. Serve them after dinner with dessert or a blue cheese assortment, OR toss it in a margarita like I did and marvel at its versatility.

Tawny ports are a blend of wines that have been aged longer than their ruby brethren. This extra exposure to the barrels allows just a hint of oxygen to enter the wine, giving it the amber color it is famous for. Tawnies tend to be sweeter than rubies, and feature more toasty, cooked fruit flavors. When it comes to cocktails, you can treat tawny ports like a rich simple syrup.

Pineapple Upside-Down Margarita

YIELD: 1 DRINK

These flavors are not limited to a cake anymore. The next step is figuring out how to serve this upside-down.

INGREDIENTS

1 Combine the sea salt and brown sugar in a small dish. Wet the rim of a margarita coupe and dip the rim into the mixture.

2 Add the tequila, mezcal, Luxardo, pineapple nectar, lime juice, agave nectar, and ice to a Boston Shaker. Shake until combined and well-chilled.

3 Strain the cocktail into the margarita coupe, garnish with the maraschino cherry and the grilled pineapple wedge, and serve.

- 1½ oz. tequila reposado
- ¾ oz. mezcal
- ¾ oz. of Luxardo
- 1 oz. pineapple nectar
- ½ oz. freshly squeezed lime juice
- ½ oz. agave nectar
- 1 tablespoon sea salt
- 1 tablespoon brown sugar
- Maraschino cherry for garnish
- Grilled pineapple wedge for garnish

Chocolate Espresso Margarita

This one's great for a pick-me-up at the start of the evening, but it also works well as a dessert or nightcap.

INGREDIENTS

½ oz. coffee tequila

1 oz. tequila plata

½ oz. orange liqueur

1 oz. espresso or strong coffee, chilled

2 oz. heavy cream

Cocoa powder for the rim

Chocolate shavings for garnish

1 twist of orange for garnish

1 Add the heavy cream to a Boston Shaker and shake until it has thickened but is not the consistency of whipped cream.

2 Rinse out one end of the Boston Shaker. Add the tequilas, the orange liqueur, espresso, and ice, and stir until combined and well-chilled.

3 Wet the rim of a martini glass or margarita coupe and dip it into the cocoa powder. Strain the cocktail into the glass and then float the cream on top. Sprinkle chocolate shavings on top, garnish with the twist of orange, and serve.

Variation: For a slightly different spin on this one, try using white chocolate components.

The Shot

The old standby. One tequila, two tequila, three tequila, floor . . .

1 Pour tequila into a tall shot glass.

2 Lick the back of one hand and sprinkle salt on it. Lick the salt off, drink the tequila, and then bite down on the lime wedge.

INGREDIENTS

1½ oz. tequila

1 wedge of lime

Sea salt

Margarita Jello Shots

Jello shots are whimsical and easy to transport, which is why I love bringing them to parties! They are also versatile, as you can make almost any version of a cocktail into a jello shot. If you are feeling extra crafty, you can put tiny wedges of lime on the edge of each cup.

INGREDIENTS

3 oz. packet of lime-flavored gelatin

½ cup boiling water

½ cup boiling apple juice

3 oz. tequila plata

2 oz. orange liqueur (Triple Sec, Cointreau, or Grand Marnier)

1 oz. lime juice

¼ cup cold water

Sea salt for the rim

Small lime wedges, optional

1 Combine the cold water, lime juice, tequila, and orange liqueur in a mixing bowl and place the bowl in the refrigerator.

2 Pour the package of lime gelatin into a large bowl. Add the apple juice and boiling water, and stir until completely dissolved. Remove the other bowl from the refrigerator and add its contents to the gelatin mixture.

3 Wet the rims of shot glasses or condiment cups and then dip the rims in sea salt. Pour the mixture into each individual container, and refrigerate for anywhere from three hours to overnight.

Frozen

Frozen beverages first rose to prominence in the United States during the 1950s, when people everywhere started to find that the margarita and its frozen kin were the perfect way to spend their leisure time—whether it be the beach or a back yard barbeque. Most people use blenders to make the frozen margarita, but if you are going to be cranking them out for the public, it might be wise to invest in a slushy machine.

The Original Frozen Margarita

YIELD: 1 DRINK

These frozen treats churn around in those iconic slushy machines at island resorts and margarita bars. Lucky for you, frozen margaritas are easy to make in a household blender.

1 Combine all ingredients, save the sea salt and lime wedge, in a blender and blend until there are no large pieces.

2 Rub the wedge of lime around the edge of a margarita coupe and dip the rim into the salt. Pour contents of blender into the glass, garnish with the lime wedge, and serve.

INGREDIENTS

3 oz. tequila plata

1½ oz. freshly squeezed lime juice

1 oz. simple syrup

1½ oz. orange liqueur (Triple Sec, Cointreau, or Grand Marnier)

1 cup ice

Sea salt for the rim

1 wedge of lime for the rim

Coconut Margarita

YIELD: 1 DRINK

Reminiscent of a piña colada, this frozen concoction will transport you directly to a tropical beach. For extra flavor, add some toasted coconut to the top of the drink!

INGREDIENTS

2 oz. tequila anejo

2 oz. coconut puree

1 oz. freshly squeezed lime juice

¼ oz. agave nectar

½ oz. orange liqueur (Triple Sec, Cointreau, or Grand Marnier)

1 cup ice

Sea salt for the rim

Lime wedge for the rim

1 Crush ice in a blender. Add tequila, coconut puree, lime juice, agave nectar, and orange liqueur. Blend for a few seconds or until everything is combined.

2 Rub the lime wedge on the rim of a martini glass or margarita coupe and then dip the rim in salt. Pour the contents of the blender into the glass, garnish with the lime wedge, and serve.

Honeydew Melon and Mint Margarita

YIELD: 1 DRINK

Honeydew melons, when just slightly overripe, tend to be sweet. Try cutting that sweetness with some mint. The mint tempers it just enough to allow the melon's brightness to shine.

1 Combine all ingredients save the sea salt and sprig of mint in a blender and blend until there are no large pieces.

2 Wet the rim of a martini glass and then dip it into the salt. Pour the contents of the blender into the glass, garnish with the sprig of mint, and serve.

INGREDIENTS

3 oz. tequila plata

¾ cup fresh honeydew melon, diced

4–5 mint leaves

2 oz. freshly squeezed lime juice

1 oz. orange liqueur (Triple Sec, Cointreau, or Grand Marnier)

¾ cup ice

Sea salt for the rim

1 sprig of mint for garnish

Cantaloupe Basil Margarita

YIELD: 1 DRINK

This one is the perfect cocktail to take in the sunset with—the anise flavor provided by the basil pairs well with the creamy, tropical qualities of the cantaloupe.

INGREDIENTS

3 oz. tequila reposado

¾ cup fresh cantaloupe, diced

3–4 basil leaves

2 oz. freshly squeezed lime juice

1 oz. orange liqueur (Triple Sec, Cointreau, or Grand Marnier)

¾ cup ice

Sea salt for the rim

1 sprig of basil for garnish

1 Combine all ingredients save the sea salt and sprig of basil in a blender and blend until there are no large pieces.

2 Wet the rim of a margarita coupe and dip it into the sea salt. Pour contents of blender into the glass, garnish with the sprig of basil, and serve.

Kiwi Margarita

The bright green look of this one will make everyone around you jealous of your skills behind the bar.

1 Combine all ingredients save the sea salt and the lime wedge in a blender and blend until there are no large pieces.

2 Rub the wedge of lime around the rim of a margarita coupe and then dip the rim into sea salt. Pour contents of blender into the glass, garnish with the lime wedge or a slice of kiwi, and serve.

INGREDIENTS

3 oz. tequila reposado

1½ oz. freshly squeezed lime juice

½ cup ripe kiwi, diced

1 oz. simple syrup

1½ oz. orange liqueur (Triple Sec, Cointreau, or Grand Marnier)

1 cup ice

Sea salt for the rim

1 wedge of lime for the rim

1 slice of kiwi for garnish, optional

Frozée Margarita (Rosé All Day)

YIELD: 1 DRINK

I like Provencal or South African rosé for this recipe. Rosé from these regions tends to be light, dry, and crisp. Drink this one all summer long (or, like me, every season!)

INGREDIENTS

2½ oz. tequila plata

¼ cup of your favorite rosé wine

2 oz. freshly squeezed lime juice

1 oz. orange liqueur (Triple Sec, Cointreau, or Grand Marnier)

1 cup ice

Pink Himalayan or Hawaiian sea salt for the rim

1 wedge of lime for the rim

1 Combine all ingredients save the salt and wedge of lime in a blender and blend until there are no large pieces.

2 Rub the lime over the rim of a margarita coupe and dip the rim into sea salt. Pour contents of blender into the glass, garnish with the wedge of lime, and serve.

Watermelon Basil

Try to find baby basil for this one. Larger, more mature basil can be quite strong and licorice-y, which doesn't always fit everyone's palate. I prefer to use baby basil, which is much more delicate and minty than its older brother.

1 Combine all ingredients save the sea salt and wedge of lime in a blender and blend until there are no large pieces.

2 Rub the wedge of lime around the edge of a margarita coupe and dip the rim into the salt. Pour contents of blender into the glass, garnish with the lime wedge, and serve.

INGREDIENTS

3 oz. tequila plata

1½ oz. freshly squeezed lime juice

1 cup fresh watermelon, diced

3–4 basil leaves

1 oz. simple syrup

1½ oz. orange liqueur (Triple Sec, Cointreau, or Grand Marnier)

1 cup ice

Sea salt for the rim

1 wedge of lime for the rim

The Hawaiian (Passion Fruit)

This can be easily transformed into a margarita on the rocks if you don't dig the frozen version. Just remove the ice and mix in a cocktail shaker.

INGREDIENTS

3 oz. tequila reposado

3 oz. passion fruit nectar

1 oz. freshly squeezed lime juice

½ oz. orange liqueur (Triple Sec, Cointreau, or Grand Marnier)

½ oz. agave nectar

1 cup ice

Sea salt for the rim

1 wedge of lime for the rim

1 Combine all ingredients save the sea salt and the lime wedge in a blender and blend until there are no large pieces.

2 Rub the wedge of lime around the edge of a margarita coupe and dip the rim into the salt. Pour contents of blender into the glass, garnish with the lime wedge, and serve.

Variation: For an added burst of green and freshness, add a sprig of mint to this one at the very end.

Frozen Pineapple Margarita

YIELD: 1 DRINK

If you want to experiment with this one, try grilling the pineapple. The caramelized sugars and hint of smoke add another layer of complexity to this frozen delight.

1 Combine all ingredients save the sea salt and wedge of lime in a blender and blend until there are no large pieces.

2 Rub the wedge of lime around the edge of a margarita coupe and dip the rim into the salt. Pour contents of blender into the glass, garnish with the lime wedge, and serve.

INGREDIENTS

2 oz. tequila plata

1 oz. mezcal

3 oz. pineapple juice

1 cup ice

¼ cup fresh pineapple, cubed

1½ oz. orange liqueur
(Triple Sec, Cointreau,
or Grand Marnier)

2 oz. freshly squeezed lime juice

Sea salt for the rim

1 wedge of lime for the rim

Strawberry and Orange Frozen Margarita

YIELD: 1 DRINK

It's tempting to take this shortcut, but using freshly squeezed orange juice instead of the kind that comes in a bottle makes a huge difference in every kind of margarita, as the flavor it provides is brighter and cleaner.

INGREDIENTS

3 oz. tequila plata

1 oz. freshly squeezed lime juice

1½ oz. freshly squeezed orange juice

½ cup fresh strawberries, diced

1 oz. simple syrup

1½ oz. orange liqueur (Triple Sec, Cointreau, or Grand Marnier)

1 cup ice

Sea salt for the rim

1 wedge of orange for the rim

1 small strawberry for garnish, optional

1 Combine all ingredients save the sea salt and wedge of orange in a blender and blend until there are no large pieces.

2 Rub the wedge of orange around the edge of a margarita coupe and dip the rim into the salt. Pour contents of blender into the glass, garnish with the orange wedge or a small strawberry, and serve.

Pineapple and Tamarind Frozen Margarita

YIELD: 1 DRINK

Tamarind is a unique flavor that I love! In this cocktail it accentuates the sweetness of the pineapple, providing your taste buds with a true adventure.

INGREDIENTS

3 oz. tequila reposado

3 oz. pineapple juice

¼ cup fresh pineapple, cubed

1 oz. tamarind nectar

1 oz. orange liqueur (Triple Sec, Cointreau, or Grand Marnier)

2 oz. freshly squeezed lime juice

1 cup ice

Sea salt for the rim

1 wedge of pineapple for the rim

1 Combine all ingredients save the sea salt and the wedge of pineapple in a blender and blend until there are no large pieces.

2 Rub the wedge of pineapple around the edge of a margarita coupe and dip the rim into the salt. Pour contents of blender into the glass, garnish with the pineapple wedge, and serve.

Tip: Nervous about where you can find tamarind nectar? Don't be! Almost any grocery store will carry it, and Goya offers a solid one.

Apple Cinnamon Frozen Margarita

YIELD: 1 DRINK

What to do with all those apples you just picked at the orchard? Some people make pies and crisps. I make margaritas.

1 To make the simple syrup: See simple syrup recipe on Page 15. When syrup is boiling, add two cinnamon sticks. After one minute, remove the saucepan from the heat and allow the cinnamon stick to cool with the syrup.

2 Combine the sugar, cinnamon, and sea salt in a small bowl and set aside.

3 Combine the mezcal, tequila, apple cider, lemon juice, cinnamon-infused simple syrup, orange liqueur, and ice in a blender and blend until there are no large chunks.

4 Rub the lemon wedge around the rim of a margarita coupe and then dip the rim in the cinnamon-sugar-salt mixture. Pour contents of the blender into the glass, garnish with the cinnamon stick, and serve.

INGREDIENTS

1½ oz. mezcal

1 oz. tequila plata

½ cup fresh apple cider

1 oz. freshly squeezed lemon juice

1 oz. cinnamon-infused simple syrup

½ oz. orange liqueur (Triple Sec, Cointreau, or Grand Marnier)

¾ cup ice

1 teaspoon sea salt

1 tablespoon sugar

1 teaspoon cinnamon

1 wedge of lemon for the rim

1 cinnamon stick for garnish

Orange Coconut

Try toasting some coconut flakes to grind up and use to mix in with the salt for the rim. This will add an extra layer of flavor that will make this cocktail stand out.

1 Add ice to a blender and crush. Add tequila, coconut puree, orange juice, lime juice, agave nectar, and orange liqueur. Blend until there are no large chunks of ice.

2 Rub the wedge of lime around the edge of a margarita coupe and dip the rim into the salt. Pour contents of blender into the glass, garnish with the twist of orange peel, and serve.

INGREDIENTS

2½ oz. tequila anejo

2 oz. coconut puree

2 oz. freshly squeezed orange juice

½ oz. freshly squeezed lime juice

1 cup ice

½ oz. agave nectar

1 oz. orange liqueur (Triple Sec, Cointreau, or Grand Marnier)

Sea salt for the rim

1 wedge of lime for the rim

1 twist of orange

Spicy

I have been a spicy food lover for a long time now, and once you get into the world of spicy food you can never really go back. But I only recently discovered that my beloved heat was not limited to food. There are spicy drinks! This may be my favorite section in the entire book, because to my taste buds, spice is flavor. If you're a little wary of venturing into this part, here's some great news—you can easily control how much spice goes into your drink. If spicy isn't your thing, I recommend cutting the spicy ingredients by half. And if you're one of those people who can't get enough, then by all means add as many chilies or as much hot sauce as you damn well please.

Ancho Chili Margarita

YIELD: 1 DRINK

Ancho chilies are the dried version of poblano peppers. Think of it like a cross between a jalapeño and a bell pepper. Not too spicy, but still with a nice kick. If you are looking to get into the spicy cocktail world, this is a great place to start.

INGREDIENTS

- 2 oz. tequila reposado
- 1 oz. ancho chili-infused simple syrup
- 1 oz. freshly squeezed lime juice
- ¾ oz. orange liqueur (Triple Sec, Cointreau, or Grand Marnier)
- 1 tablespoon smoked sea salt
- ½ teaspoon chili powder
- 1 wedge of lime for the rim

1 To make the simple syrup: See simple syrup recipe on Page 15. When syrup is boiling, add two whole dried ancho chilies. After one minute, remove the saucepan from the heat and allow the chilies to cool with the syrup.

2 To make the rub for the chili rim: Combine the smoked sea salt and chili powder in a small dish and set aside.

3 Fill a Boston Shaker about halfway with ice. Add tequila, ancho chili-infused syrup, lime juice, and orange liqueur, and shake vigorously until well-combined.

4 Rub the lime or lemon wedge around the rim of a rocks glass and then dip the rim in the chili powder-salt mixture. Fill the glass to the top with ice and strain the margarita into the glass. Place the wedge of lime on the rim and serve!

TIP: Be very careful when handling the hot chili peppers in some of these recipes. Be sure to wash your hands, knives, and cutting surfaces very well after using the peppers, and avoid touching your eyes for a few hours. Trust me, I've been there one too many times and hot pepper eyes are NOT fun. Habaneros are particularly potent, so take extra care with those recipes that call for them. This is a warning, but don't let it deter you from using the hot peppers! Those that utilize them are some of my favorites in this entire book.

Cucumber Jalapeño Margarita

YIELD: 1 DRINK

This one's fresh and spicy, and perfect for summer. I'm a spice fanatic, but I love how the cucumber instantly cools my mouth down from the spicy jalapeño.

1 To make the simple syrup: See simple syrup recipe on Page 15. When syrup is boiling, add a diced jalapeño pepper. After one minute, remove the saucepan from the heat and allow the jalapeño to cool with the syrup.

2 Add the tequila, one heaping tablespoon of cucumber, and 2–3 slices of fresh jalapeño to a Boston Shaker and muddle. Add ice, lime juice, and simple syrup, and shake until combined.

3 Rub the lime wedge around the rim of a rocks glass and then dip it in the salt. Fill the glass with ice and strain margarita into the glass. Garnish with the lime wedge, any leftover cucumber and/or jalapeño, and serve!

INGREDIENTS

4 oz. tequila reposado

2 oz. freshly squeezed lime juice

2 oz. jalapeño-infused simple syrup or agave nectar

1 jalapeño, cut into thin disks

1¼ tablespoons cucumber, diced

Salt for the rim

1 wedge of lime for the rim

Jalapeño Pineapple Margarita

YIELD: 1 DRINK

If you can't take the heat, add some sweet! This pleasantly spicy combo works because of the contrasting flavors. By mixing the perfect amount of each component, you will create a well-balanced margarita that offers the best of both worlds.

INGREDIENTS

4 oz. tequila reposado

2 oz. freshly squeezed lime juice

1 oz. jalapeño-infused simple syrup or agave nectar

1 oz. pineapple juice

2–3 thin slices of jalapeño

1¼ tablespoons pineapple, diced

Sea salt for the rim

1 wedge of lime for the rim

1 To make the simple syrup: See simple syrup recipe on Page 15. When syrup is boiling, add a diced jalapeño pepper. After one minute, remove the saucepan from the heat and allow the jalapeño to cool with the syrup.

2 Add the tequila, 1 heaping tablespoon of pineapple, and 2–3 slices of jalapeño to a Boston Shaker and muddle. Add ice, lime juice, simple syrup, and pineapple juice, and shake until well-combined.

3 Rub the lime wedge around the rim of a rocks glass and then dip it in the salt. Fill glass with ice and strain margarita into glass. Garnish with a lime wedge and any remaining pineapple or jalapeño, and then serve.

TIP: Infused tequilas are interesting!! Pour your favorite tequila plata over chopped pineapple, watermelon, strawberries, jalapeños, or any herb you like. Seal the container and let it sit in a cool, dark spot for anywhere from two days to a week. Check on it after the first two days and then every day after that to monitor the flavor. Once it suits your taste, your home-infused tequila is ready for sipping or mixing. And remember not to toss out your infusing agent! Instead, remove and save it for future cocktails!

Matcha Margarita

Matcha! The green tea that is all the rage. Everyone is going to matcha bars, making matcha desserts, and now I am even concocting matcha margs! This green tea is leafy and grassy, with a hint of citrus. It is what all the health nuts are after and clearly I am one of them.

1 Combine the salt and two teaspoons of the matcha powder. Wet the rim of a rocks glass with some lime juice and dip the glass into the matcha-and-salt mixture.

2 Add the jalapeño and lime juice to a Boston Shaker and muddle until the pepper breaks down and releases its flavor. Add the tequila, green tea, simple syrup, orange liqueur, remaining matcha powder, and ice to the shaker and shake until well-chilled.

3 Fill the rocks glass with ice and strain the cocktail into the glass. Garnish with 2–3 fresh jalapeño rings and serve.

INGREDIENTS

2 oz. tequila plata

3 oz. freshly brewed, chilled green tea

1 oz. freshly squeezed lime juice

½ oz. simple syrup

½ oz. orange liqueur (Triple Sec, Cointreau, or Grand Marnier)

½ inch piece of fresh jalapeño

2¼ teaspoons matcha powder

1 teaspoon fine sea salt

2–3 jalapeño slices

Habanero Margarita

This may be the spiciest recipe in the book. And make sure you handle the habaneros very carefully!

INGREDIENTS

2 oz. tequila plata

1 oz. freshly squeezed lime juice

¾ oz. habanero-infused simple syrup

1 oz. orange liqueur (Triple Sec, Cointreau, or Grand Marnier)

Sea salt for the rim

1 wedge of lime for the rim

1 slice of habanero for garnish

1 basil leaf for garnish

1 To make the simple syrup: See simple syrup recipe on Page 15. When syrup is boiling, add half of a diced habanero pepper. After one minute, remove the saucepan from the heat and allow the pepper to cool with the syrup.

2 Fill a Boston Shaker about halfway with ice. Add tequila, lime juice, habanero-infused simple syrup, and orange liqueur, and shake vigorously until well-combined.

3 Rub the lime wedge around the rim of a rocks glass and then dip the rim in sea salt. Fill the glass to the top with ice and strain the margarita into the glass. Garnish with the lime wedge, slice of habanero, and basil leaf, and serve.

Variation: Looking for even more heat? Muddle a small piece of the habanero in the bottom of the shaker with the lime juice. This will be HOT!

Sriracha Margarita

YIELD: 1 DRINK

In my opinion, Sriracha is not so much spicy as it is exceptionally flavorful. When adding it to any dish, I always keep the savory garlic notes that go along with its heat in mind. This margarita can almost be considered a sauce for tacos, since they go that well together.

1 Fill a Boston Shaker about halfway with ice. Add tequila, lime juice, Sriracha, simple syrup, and orange liqueur, and shake vigorously until well-combined.

2 Rub the lime wedge around the rim of a rocks glass and dip the rim in sea salt. Fill the rocks glass with ice and strain the margarita into the glass. Garnish with the wedge of lime and serve!

INGREDIENTS

2 oz. tequila plata

1 oz. freshly squeezed lime juice

1 teaspoon Sriracha hot sauce

¾ oz. simple syrup

1 oz. orange liqueur (Triple Sec, Cointreau, or Grand Marnier)

Sea salt for the rim

1 wedge of lime for the rim

Michelada Margarita

YIELD: 1 DRINK

If you like Bloody Marys then you will absolutely love Micheladas. Adding some of a Bloody Mary's components to a lager creates this perfectly piquant beverage.

INGREDIENTS

1 12 oz. can of Tecate, or any lager you like will work

2 oz. tequila plata

1 oz. freshly squeezed lime juice

½ oz. orange liqueur (Triple Sec, Cointreau, or Grand Marnier)

½ oz. hot sauce

⅛ oz. Worcestershire sauce

⅛ oz. soy sauce

1 teaspoon sea salt

1 teaspoon freshly ground black pepper

1 wedge of lime for the rim

1 Combine the sea salt and pepper in a small dish and set aside. Wet the rim of a pint glass with lime juice and dip it in the salt-and-pepper mixture.

2 Combine the remaining ingredients in a Boston Shaker and stir together. Fill the glass with ice, pour contents of the shaker into the glass, and serve with the wedge of lime.

Bloody Margarita

YIELD: 1 DRINK

The Bloody Mary is my go-to brunch cocktail. But I prefer tequila to the traditional vodka, as I think the former provides more flavor. Combine the elements of a great margarita with the best parts of a Bloody Mary and kick your brunch up a notch.

1 Combine the sea salt, 1 teaspoon of the black pepper, chili powder, and celery salt in a small dish. Rub the lime wedge around the outer rim of a rocks glass and then dip the rim into the mixture.

2 Combine the tequila, orange juice, lime juice, jalapeño juice, tomato juice, hot sauce, horseradish, and remaining black pepper in a Boston Shaker. Add ice and shake until well-combined.

3 Fill the glass with ice and strain the cocktail into the glass. Garnish with the lime wedge, pickled jalapeños, and the celery stalk. Adjust the seasonings to your taste and serve.

INGREDIENTS

- 2 oz. tequila reposado
- 1 oz. freshly squeezed orange juice
- ½ oz. freshly squeezed lime juice
- ¼ oz. pickled jalapeño juice
- 2 oz. tomato juice
- Dash of hot sauce
- ⅛ teaspoon horseradish
- 1 tablespoon sea salt
- 1⅛ teaspoon freshly ground black pepper
- 1 teaspoon celery salt
- 1 teaspoon chili powder
- 1 wedge of lime for the rim
- 1 leafy stalk of celery for garnish
- Pickled jalapeños for garnish

Bloody Kimchi Margarita

Kimchi—a fermented cabbage that is seasoned with various chili powders, garlic, and ginger—is pretty widely available these days. To the uninitiated, it may sound strange. But trust me, it's delicious, and able to dress up just about anything.

INGREDIENTS

- 2 oz. tequila reposado
- 1 oz. freshly squeezed orange juice
- ½ oz. freshly squeezed lime juice
- ¼ oz. pickled jalapeño juice
- 2 oz. tomato juice
- 1½ oz. kimchi
- ⅛ teaspoon horseradish
- 1 tablespoon sea salt
- 1⅛ teaspoon freshly ground black pepper
- 1 teaspoon celery salt
- 1 teaspoon chili powder
- 1 wedge of lime for the rim
- 1 leafy stalk of celery for garnish
- 1 piece of kimchi for garnish
- Pickled jalapeños for garnish

1 Combine the sea salt, 1 teaspoon of the black pepper, chili powder, and celery salt in a small dish. Rub the lime wedge around the outer rim of a rocks glass and then dip the rim into the mixture.

2 Place the kimchi and its juice in a food processor or blender and blend until smooth.

3 Combine the tequila, orange juice, lime juice, jalapeño juice, tomato juice, kimchi puree, horseradish, and remaining black pepper in a Boston Shaker. Add ice and shake until well-combined.

4 Fill the glass with ice and strain the cocktail into the glass. Garnish with the lime wedge, pickled jalapeños, a piece of kimchi, and the celery stalk. Adjust the seasonings to your taste, and serve.

Mango Habanero Margarita

YIELD: 1 DRINK

Tropical fruits like mango crave spice, allowing its sweetness to provide a cooling effect—a must when dealing with the devilishly hot habanero.

INGREDIENTS

3 oz. tequila reposado

1 oz. freshly squeezed lime juice

2 oz. fresh mango

1 oz. orange liqueur (Triple Sec, Cointreau, or Grand Marnier)

¾ oz. habanero-infused simple syrup

1 teaspoon chili powder

1 teaspoon sea salt

1 wedge of lime for the rim

1 basil leaf for garnish

1 Add the mango to a blender or food processor and blend until smooth.

2 To make the simple syrup: See simple syrup recipe on Page 15. When syrup is boiling, add half of a diced habanero pepper. After one minute, remove the saucepan from the heat and allow the pepper to cool with the syrup.

3 Combine the chili powder and sea salt in a small dish and set aside.

4 Fill a Boston Shaker about halfway with ice. Add tequila, lime juice, mango puree, orange liqueur, and habanero-infused simple syrup, and shake vigorously until well-combined.

5 Rub the lime wedge around the rim of a rocks glass and then dip the rim into the salt-and-chili powder mixture. Fill the rocks glass with ice and strain the margarita into the glass. Garnish with the basil leaf and serve.

Serrano Chili and Mint Margarita

Serranos are hotter than jalapeños, so you'll need the mint to cool this cocktail down. But don't be scared, this combo produces a perfectly clean, refreshing beverage.

1 Add the tequila and serrano pepper to a Boston Shaker and muddle.

2 Add ice, lime juice, simple syrup, and orange liqueur to the shaker, and shake vigorously until combined and well-chilled.

3 Wet the rim of a martini glass or margarita coupe and dip into the salt. Strain the cocktail into the glass, garnish with a twist of lime or a lime wedge, top with one or two slices of the serrano pepper, and serve.

Tip: For muddling herbs, spices, and fruits in the bottom of a cocktail shaker, all you really need is a rounded, dull kitchen tool that can mash up whatever is in the cup. If you have a proper muddler, great! If not, the next best thing is the back of a wooden spoon. Grab one and muddle away!!

INGREDIENTS

2 oz. tequila plata

1 oz. freshly squeezed lime juice

¾ oz. simple syrup

½ of a serrano pepper

1 oz. orange liqueur (Triple Sec, Cointreau, or Grand Marnier)

Sea salt for the rim

Serrano chili slices for garnish

1 wedge of lime, optional

1 twist of lime, optional

Bubbly

Whether it's beer, cava, prosecco, champagne, cider, tonic, or seltzer, bubbles sell. Carbonation is whimsical and exciting, and puts everyone in the mind to celebrate and have a good time. Because of this, a sparkling cocktail can brighten up a cocktail party—or even a random weeknight. I truly don't believe I have ever seen a frown upon a person's face while they're holding a fizzy drink. It's hard to improve on the margarita's festive reputation, but adding a little extra effervescence does just that! Trust me, gilding a margarita with your favorite bubbly will invigorate any occasion.

Tex-Mex Mule

My take on the famous Moscow Mule. The flavors of the ginger beer are only enhanced by tequila. If you're looking for an excuse to utilize those copper mugs you bought, look no further than this cocktail.

1 Fill a Boston Shaker halfway with ice. Add tequila, lime juice, ginger liqueur, orange liqueur, and ginger beer, and shake until very well-chilled.

2 Rub the outer rim of a copper mug or rocks glass with the lime wedge and then dip the rim into the salt. Fill the glass with ice and strain the cocktail into it. Garnish with the lime wedge and serve.

INGREDIENTS

2½ oz. tequila reposado

2 oz. freshly squeezed lime juice

½ oz. Domaine de Canton, or other ginger-flavored liqueur

½ oz. orange liqueur (Triple Sec, Cointreau, or Grand Marnier)

5 oz. ginger beer

Sea salt for the rim

1 wedge of lime for the rim

Julep Margarita

A great take on the classic Mint Julep. Serve these during the Triple Crown races and watch your get-together jump to the next level.

INGREDIENTS

2 oz. anejo tequila

1 teaspoon powdered sugar

½ oz. seltzer

Squeeze of lime juice

4–5 mint leaves

1 sprig of mint

1 Place the mint leaves and powdered sugar in the bottom of a rocks glass and muddle until the flavors have been extracted. Add the seltzer and squeeze of lime juice, and fill glass with crushed ice.

2 Add the tequila and top with another small splash of seltzer. Stir with a bar spoon, garnish with a fresh sprig of mint, and serve!

Cava Margarita

Cava is always an affordable option in terms of sparkling wine. It is from the region of Catalonia in Spain, which contains Barcelona. Cava is made in the classic Champagne method but with the indigenous grapes of the region. The dry style of cava adds perfect fizz and fruitiness to this margarita.

1 Fill a Boston Shaker halfway with ice. Add tequila, lime juice, simple syrup, and orange liqueur, and shake until well-chilled.

2 Wet the rim of a champagne flute and dip it into the sea salt. Strain cocktail into the glass, top with cava, garnish with the lime wedge, and serve.

INGREDIENTS

2 oz. tequila plata

1 oz. freshly squeezed lime juice

¾ oz. simple syrup

1 oz. orange liqueur (Triple Sec, Cointreau, or Grand Marnier)

6 oz. cava

Sea salt for the rim

1 wedge of lime for the rim

Coronarita

These are all over bar menus of late. And it's easy to see why—who doesn't want an entire beer chilling in their margarita?

INGREDIENTS

2 oz. tequila plata

1 oz. freshly squeezed lime juice

¾ oz. simple syrup

1 oz. orange liqueur (Triple Sec, Cointreau, or Grand Marnier)

1 7 oz. mini-bottle of Corona

Sea salt for the rim

1 wedge of lime for the rim

1 Fill a Boston Shaker halfway with ice. Add tequila, lime juice, simple syrup, and orange liqueur, and shake until well-combined.

2 Rub the lime wedge around the rim of a rocks glass and dip the rim in sea salt. Fill the glass with ice and strain the margarita into the glass. Garnish with the lime wedge, carefully flip the mini-bottle of Corona into the glass, and serve!

Hard Apple Cider Margarita

YIELD: 1 DRINK

Hard apple cider is great on its own. Pair it with some tequila and ginger, and you're living large!

1 Fill a Boston Shaker halfway with ice. Add tequila, lime juice, ginger liqueur, and orange liqueur, and shake until well-combined.

2 Rub the lime wedge around the rim of a rocks glass and dip the rim in sea salt. Fill the rocks glass with ice and strain the margarita into the glass. Garnish with the lime wedge, carefully flip the bottle of cider into the glass, and serve!

INGREDIENTS

2 oz. tequila plata

1 oz. freshly squeezed lime juice

¾ oz. Domaine de Canton, or other ginger-flavored liqueur

1 oz. orange liqueur (Triple Sec, Cointreau, or Grand Marnier)

1 12 oz. bottle of hard apple cider

Sea salt for the rim

1 wedge of lime for the rim

Blackberry Sage Margarita

Tart and herbaceous, this margarita has it all. Sage has such a unique flavor that you will even impress yourself with this fun cocktail!

INGREDIENTS

2½ oz. tequila plata

1 oz. freshly squeezed lime juice

1 oz. simple syrup

4–5 blackberries

2–3 sage leaves

Sea salt for the rim

1 wedge of lime for the rim

Splash of seltzer

1 sage leaf for garnish

1 Add the tequila, blackberries, and sage leaves to a Boston Shaker and muddle.

2 Add ice, lime juice, and simple syrup to the shaker, and shake vigorously until well-combined.

3 Rub the lime wedge around the rim of a rocks glass and dip the rim in sea salt. Fill the rocks glass with ice and strain the margarita into the glass. Top with the splash of seltzer, garnish with the lime wedge and a sage leaf, and serve.

Dark and Stormy Margarita

YIELD: 1 DRINK

I love the Dark and Stormy cocktail, but I also clearly love margaritas. Choosing between them got too tough, so I created the perfect crossover drink!

INGREDIENTS

2 oz. tequila reposado

¾ oz. amaro

¾ oz. freshly squeezed lime juice

2–3 dashes of orange bitters

2 oz. ginger beer

Sea salt for the rim

1 Fill a Boston Shaker about halfway with ice. Add all ingredients save the sea salt to the shaker and shake until combined and well-chilled.

2 Wet the rim of a tall glass and then dip the rim in the salt. Fill glass with ice and strain the cocktail into the glass. Top with an extra splash of ginger beer and serve!

Ginger Beer Margarita

I prefer to use extra spicy ginger beer made with real, fresh ginger root. This amplifies the flavors in the cocktail and will have your guests asking what you did to create this fierce margarita.

1 Fill a Boston Shaker about halfway with ice. Add tequila, lime juice, ginger liqueur, and orange liqueur, and shake vigorously until well-combined.

2 Rub the lime wedge around the rim of a rocks glass and dip the rim in sea salt. Fill the rocks glass with ice and strain the margarita into the glass. Garnish with the lime wedge, carefully flip the ginger beer into the glass, and serve!

INGREDIENTS

2 oz. tequila plata

1 oz. freshly squeezed lime juice

¾ oz. Domaine de Canton, or other ginger-flavored liqueur

1 oz. orange liqueur (Triple Sec, Cointreau, or Grand Marnier)

1 12 oz. bottle of ginger beer

Sea salt for the rim

1 wedge of lime for the rim

The High Roller

YIELD: 1 DRINK

This cocktail will require some serious coin. But if you are looking to impress someone, or simply treat yourself, turn to this ultra-premium, bubbly margarita.

1 Fill a Boston Shaker about halfway with ice. Add tequila, Grand Marnier, and lime juice, and shake vigorously until well-combined.

2 Rub the lime wedge around the rim of a rocks glass and dip the rim in the fleur de sel. Fill the rocks glass with ice and strain the margarita into the glass. Turn the split of champagne into the margarita, garnish with the twist of lime, and serve!

INGREDIENTS

2 oz. premium tequila plata

1 oz. Grand Marnier

1 oz. freshly squeezed lime juice

1 split of your favorite champagne (187 ml)

Fleur de sel for the rim

1 twist of lime for garnish

Think Pink

YIELD: 1 DRINK

Whether you call it "rosé" or "bro-sé," everyone is thinking pink. Rosé is a crowd-pleaser, and so is this margarita. The fruity and herbaceous qualities of the rosé elevate the tequila—as do the bubbles.

INGREDIENTS

2 oz. tequila plata

1 oz. freshly squeezed lime juice

1 oz. freshly squeezed pink grapefruit juice

3 oz. sparkling rosé wine

¾ oz. simple syrup

1 oz. orange liqueur (Triple Sec, Cointreau, Grand Marnier)

Pink Himalayan or Hawaiian sea salt for the rim

1 wedge of lime, optional

1 twist of lime, optional

1 Fill a Boston Shaker about halfway with ice. Place all of the ingredients, save the salt and lime wedge, into the shaker, and shake vigorously until combined and well-chilled.

2 Wet the rim of a martini glass or margarita coupe and dip into the salt. Strain the cocktail into the glass, garnish with a twist of lime or a lime wedge, top with one more splash of that sparkling rosé, and serve.

Tip: Don't be afraid to try different kinds of salts and spices for the rim of your margarita's glass. Plain old sea salt will always work fine, but there are also pink Himalayan and Hawaiian salts, black Icelandic salt, smoked sea salt, fleur de sel, and sel gris. Each of these will bring different flavors and aesthetic qualities to your margarita. For the margaritas that require a sugar rim, try switching it up between granulated, turbinado, light and dark brown sugar, and powdered sugar. You can also try muddling an herb or spice with the sugar to see if they will enhance your cocktail.

Ginger Ale Margarita

Use ginger ale that contains real, fresh ginger. This will make for a more flavorful margarita.

1 Fill a Boston shaker about halfway with ice. Add tequila, lime juice, ginger liqueur, and orange liqueur, and shake vigorously until well-combined.

2 Rub the lime wedge around the rim of a rocks glass and dip the rim in sea salt. Fill the rocks glass with ice and strain the margarita into the glass. Flip the bottle of ginger ale into the glass, garnish with the lime wedge, and serve.

INGREDIENTS

2 oz. tequila plata

1 oz. freshly squeezed lime juice

¾ oz. Domaine de Canton, or other ginger-flavored liqueur

1 oz. orange liqueur (Triple Sec, Cointreau, or Grand Marnier)

1 12 oz. bottle of ginger ale

Sea salt for the rim

1 wedge of lime for the rim

Mocktails

Offering an alcohol-free option other than water or soda is essential at any party. The beauty of these recipes is that they make for thirst-quenching juices, smoothies, or fun drinks for everyone to enjoy.

As much as I love a great cocktail, there are those times where I just do not want alcohol. Flavored seltzer waters or tonics are sufficient substitutes for the alcohol components in the recipes. The following drinks are kid-friendly, perfect for designated drivers, or for those poor souls who don't like tequila!

Pomegranate Mocktail

Pomegranate is high in antioxidants and perfectly tart. That's a good start for any mocktail, but its attractive, deep red color makes it a guaranteed winner.

1 Fill a Boston Shaker about halfway with ice. Add the pomegranate juice, lime juice, orange juice, and simple syrup, and shake vigorously until well-combined.

2 Rub the lime wedge around the rim of a rocks glass and dip the rim in sea salt. Fill the glass with ice and strain the contents of the shaker into the glass. Garnish with the lime wedge and pomegranate seeds, and serve.

INGREDIENTS

3 oz. pomegranate juice

2 oz. freshly squeezed lime juice

1 oz. freshly squeezed orange juice

$2/3$ oz. simple syrup

Sea salt for the rim

1 wedge of lime for the rim

Pomegranate seeds for garnish

Frozen Passion Fruit Mocktail

This one is so fun and beautiful, no one will notice that the tequila's missing.

INGREDIENTS

3 oz. lemon-lime seltzer

3 oz. passion fruit nectar

1 oz. freshly squeezed lime juice

½ oz. freshly squeezed orange juice

½ oz. agave nectar

1 cup ice

Sea salt for the rim

1 wedge of lime for garnish, optional

1 sprig of mint for garnish, optional

1 Combine all ingredients save the sea salt and wedge of lime in a blender and blend until smooth.

2 Wet the rim of a margarita glass and dip it into the sea salt. Pour the contents of the blender into the glass, garnish with the wedge of lime or a small sprig of mint, and serve.

Matcha Mockarita

YIELD: 1 DRINK

This mocktail is so healthy you can taste the green! Yes, that may sound impossible, but once you try it you'll see what I mean.

1 Combine the sea salt and two teaspoons of the matcha powder in a small dish. Rub the rim of a rocks glass with the wedge of lime and then dip the rim into the matcha-and-salt mixture.

2 Add the jalapeño pepper and the lime juice to a Boston Shaker and muddle. When the pepper is broken down, add the ginger tea, green tea, orange juice, remaining matcha powder, and ice, and shake until well-chilled.

3 Fill the rocks glass with ice and strain the contents of the shaker into the glass. Garnish with the jalapeño rings and serve.

INGREDIENTS

2 oz. freshly brewed ginger tea, chilled

3 oz. freshly brewed green tea, chilled

1 oz. freshly squeezed lime juice

½ oz. simple syrup

½ oz. freshly squeezed orange juice

2 ¼ teaspoons matcha powder

½ inch piece of jalapeño

1 teaspoon sea salt for the rim

1 wedge of lime for the rim

2–3 jalapeño rings for garnish

Frozen Kiwi Mocktail

YIELD: 1 DRINK

This fun, green margarita will remind you just how much you love kiwi!

INGREDIENTS

3 oz. apple juce

1½ oz. freshly squeezed lime juice

½ cup ripe kiwi, diced

1 oz. simple syrup

1½ oz. freshly squeezed orange juice

1 cup ice

Sea salt for the rim

1 wedge of lime for the rim

1 slice of kiwi for the rim, optional

1 Place all ingredients save the sea salt, wedge of lime, and slice of kiwi in a blender and blend until no large ice chunks remain.

2 Rub the lime wedge around the edge of a margarita glass and then dip the rim in the salt. Pour the contents of the blender into the glass, garnish with the wedge of lime or slice of kiwi, and serve.

Cucumber Mint Mocktail

YIELD: 1 DRINK

Mint and cucumber are two of my favorite flavors during the summer. This fizzy drink always takes me there, no matter how frigid it is outdoors.

1 To make the simple syrup: See simple syrup recipe on Page 15. When syrup is boiling, add six mint leaves. After one minute, remove the saucepan from the heat and allow the mint to cool with the syrup.

2 Add the cucumber and 2–3 mint leaves to a Boston Shaker and muddle. Add lime juice, mint-infused simple syrup, and ice to the shaker, and shake until well-combined.

3 Rub the lime wedge around the rim of a rocks glass and dip the rim in sea salt. Fill the rocks glass with ice and strain the contents of the shaker into the glass. Add the tonic water and stir. Garnish with the wedge of lime and mint leaves, and serve.

INGREDIENTS

4 oz. tonic water

2 oz. freshly squeezed lime juice

2 oz. mint-infused simple syrup or agave nectar

10–12 mint leaves

1 tablespoon cucumber, diced

Sea salt for the rim

1 wedge of lime for the rim

Lemon-Lime Spritz

I first thought of this mocktail while trying to create a homemade version of Sprite. I wanted something less sugary, so that I could have two or three glasses and not feel guilty!

INGREDIENTS

4 oz. lemon-lime soda or seltzer

½ oz. freshly squeezed lime juice

½ oz. freshly squeezed lemon juice

1 oz. simple syrup

Sea salt for the rim

1 wedge of lime for the rim

1 wedge of lemon for the rim

1 Fill a Boston Shaker about halfway with ice. Add lime juice, lemon juice, and simple syrup, and shake vigorously until well-combined.

2 Rub the lime or lemon wedge around the rim of a rocks glass and then dip the rim in sea salt. Fill the glass with ice and strain the contents of the shaker into the glass. Add the lemon-lime soda or seltzer and stir. Garnish with the lime and/or lemon wedge, and serve.

Chocolate Espresso Mocktail

YIELD: 1 DRINK

The best part about this mocktail is the extra-sweet treat once you finished. Crunching on the chocolate-covered espresso beans that made for such a beautiful garnish is both delicious and devilish.

1 Make the espresso or coffee. While it is still hot, stir in the honey and then place in the refrigerator.

2 Add the heavy cream to a Boston Shaker and shake until it has thickened but is not the consistency of whipped cream.

3 Rinse out one end of the Boston Shaker. Add the espresso, chocolate syrup, and ice, and stir until combined and chilled.

4 Wet the rim of a martini glass or margarita coupe and dip it into the cocoa powder. Strain the contents of the shaker into the glass and then float the cream on top. Sprinkle the chocolate-covered espresso beans on top, garnish with the twist of orange, and serve.

INGREDIENTS

3 oz. espresso or strong coffee

1 teaspoon honey

1 teaspoon chocolate syrup

2 oz. heavy cream

Cocoa powder for the rim

2–3 chocolate-covered espresso beans for garnish

1 twist of orange for garnish

Mango-Lime Margarita

YIELD: 1 DRINK

The combination of mango and lime is powerful enough to whisk your taste buds away to a tropical paradise.

INGREDIENTS

3 oz. fresh mango

2 oz. freshly squeezed orange juice

2 oz. freshly squeezed lime juice

2 oz. seltzer

1 teaspoon chili powder

1 teaspoon sea salt

1 wedge of lime for the rim

1 basil leaf for garnish

1 Place the mango in a blender and blend until it has been pureed.

2 Combine the sea salt and chili powder in a small dish and set aside.

3 Fill a Boston Shaker about halfway with ice. Add the mango puree, orange juice, and lime juice to the shaker, and shake vigorously until well-combined.

4 Rub the lime wedge around the rim of a rocks glass and dip the rim in the sea salt-chili powder mixture. Fill the rocks glass with ice and strain the contents of the shaker into the glass. Top with the seltzer, garnish with the basil leaf, and serve.

The Brunch Mocktail

As much as I love a boozy brunch, sometimes I'm just not in the mood. On those days, I like the flavors offered by this concoction, which is light and refreshing.

1 Combine the tonic, orange marmalade, lime juice, orange juice, and simple syrup in a Boston Shaker. Add ice and shake until well-combined.

2 Rub the lime wedge around the rim of a rocks glass and dip the rim in sea salt. Fill the rocks glass with ice and strain the contents of the shaker into the glass. Top with a splash of seltzer, garnish with the lime wedge or an orange twist, and serve!

INGREDIENTS

2 oz. tonic water

2 teaspoons orange marmalade

1 oz. freshly squeezed lime juice

½ oz. freshly squeezed orange juice

½ oz. simple syrup

Sea salt for the rim

1 wedge of lime for the rim

Splash of seltzer

1 twist of orange, optional

Index

About the Author

Author of *Dressings, Salsas and Dips,* and *Ovenless Desserts,* Mamie Fennimore has expanded her brand into the world of cocktails. With a true appreciation for and considerable knowledge of tequila and mezcal she compiled this extensive reference of margarita recipes and other unique tequila cocktails. Living and working in NYC, one of the cocktail meccas of the world, has proven to be the perfect place for inspiration and experimentation of these fun drinks!

ABOUT CIDER MILL PRESS BOOK PUBLISHERS

Good ideas ripen with time. From seed to harvest, Cider Mill
Press brings fine reading, information, and entertainment
together between the covers of its creatively crafted books.
Our Cider Mill bears fruit twice a year, publishing
a new crop of titles each spring and fall.

VISIT US ON THE WEB AT
www.cidermillpress.com

OR WRITE TO US AT
PO Box 454
12 Spring Street
Kennebunkport, Maine 04046